Global uncertainty looms as COVID-19 forces containment measures

- Global prospects are dim as the world grapples with containing the coronavirus disease (COVID-19) pandemic. The 2.9% growth realized in 2019 may be wiped out as necessary containment measures, such as local and nationwide lockdowns and travel restrictions, disrupt major sectors, especially tourism, transport, manufacturing, and trade. Latest forecasts indicate that the global economy will contract by 4.9% in 2020. Weaker demand and greater trade restrictions are expected to push down global trade volumes by 11.9% in 2020. From a 5.1% expansion in 2019, economic growth in developing Asia is seen to plummet to 0.1% this year amid sharp declines in commodity prices and tourist arrivals. The global economy could recover in 2021, but this will heavily depend on how quick and effective the global response will be in containing the pandemic.

- The Pacific subregion is expected to suffer an economic contraction because of the COVID-19 pandemic and the resultant global slowdown. The subregion's 3.7% growth in 2019 is projected to be reversed to a 4.3% contraction in 2020 as travel restrictions severely impact several tourism-dependent economies. Meanwhile, smaller economies, whose growth is driven by infrastructure projects, will be adversely affected by restrictions on the movement of labor and equipment. The subregional economy is forecast to recover in 2021, growing by 1.6%.

- The United States economy shrank at an annualized rate of 5.0% in the first quarter of 2020, the first negative growth since the first quarter of 2014. Rapid changes in demand and generally weaker economic activity amid "stay-at-home" orders by some state governments caused contractions in consumer spending, nonresidential fixed investment, exports, and inventories. Consumer spending fell by 6.8%, with durable goods spending plunging 13.2% and expenditures on services down by 9.7%. The economy is projected to contract by 5.3% this year before recovering in 2021 with an expansion of 3.8%.

- The People's Republic of China (PRC) saw its economy contract by 6.8% in the first quarter of 2020, its lowest reported quarterly performance since 1992. All primary economic drivers fell as the country implemented large-scale lockdowns to contain the spread of COVID-19. Retail sales dropped by 19.0%, while fixed-asset investment fell 16.1%. Net exports were down by 6.4%. Although most businesses have resumed work, activity remains tepid and the spread of the coronavirus overseas has resulted in a drop in demand for the PRC's exports. Full-year growth for 2020 is expected to fall to 1.8%, but to accelerate to 7.4% in 2021.

- Japan's economy slipped into recession as it contracted for the second straight quarter, with a negative annualized rate of 3.4% in the first quarter of 2020. The economy was already struggling prior to the COVID-19 pandemic as consumers absorbed a sales tax hike and the country dealt with the impact of Typhoon Hagibis in the last quarter of 2019. Private consumption, the largest component of Japan's economy, fell by 0.7%. A bleaker performance is expected in the succeeding quarters, with the government having declared a state of emergency. The economy is forecast to shrink by 5.0% in 2020 and should grow by 2.0% in 2021.

- The Australian economy grew at an annualized rate of 0.4% in the first 3 months of 2020, slightly higher than the previous quarter but below market expectations. Strong government spending on health, elderly care, and disability insurance, as well as higher exports supported the expansion. On the other hand, weak household spending and contraction in private dwelling construction have adversely affected economic performance. The containment measures taken by the government, which included both strict social distancing restrictions

GDP Growth (%, annual)

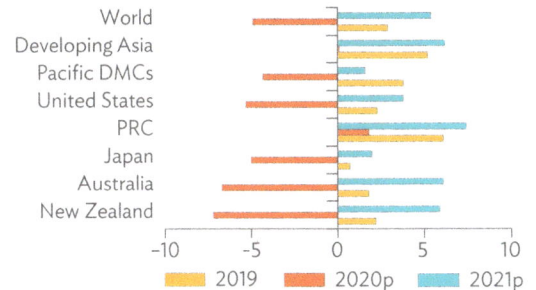

DMC = developing member country, GDP = gross domestic product, p = projection, PRC = People's Republic of China.
Notes: Developing Asia and Pacific DMCs as defined by the Asian Development Bank (ADB). Figures are based on ADB estimates except for World GDP growth.
Sources: ADB. 2020. *Asian Development Outlook 2020 Supplement: Lockdown, Loosening, and Asia's Growth Prospects.* Manila; International Monetary Fund (IMF). 2020. *World Economic Outlook April 2020: The Great Lockdown.* Washington, DC; IMF. 2020. World Economic Outlook Update June 2020. Washington, DC.

GDP Growth in Developing Asia (%, annual)

GDP = gross domestic product, p = projection.
Source: Asian Development Bank. 2020. *Asian Development Outlook 2020 Supplement: Lockdown, Loosening, and Asia's Growth Prospects.* Manila.

Timeline of lockdowns in Pacific DMC's major economic partners

DMC = developing member country, PRC = People's Republic of China.
Notes: Lockdown implementation differs significantly per country (selected areas only in Japan, the PRC, and the United States) and ranges from voluntary social distancing (Japan) to restricted mobility within a local area (e.g. Wuhan, PRC). Data as of 15 July 2020.
Sources: National government websites for coronavirus disease (COVID-19) (Australia, Japan, and New Zealand); CNN website; CBS News website; New York Times website.

Average Spot Price of Brent Crude Oil
(monthly, $/barrel)

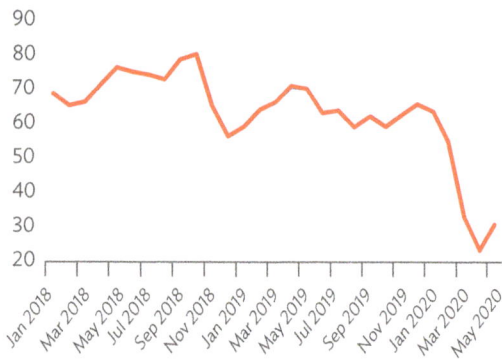

Source: World Bank Commodity Price Data (Pink Sheet).

Export Prices of Selected Commodities
(2018 = 100, annual)

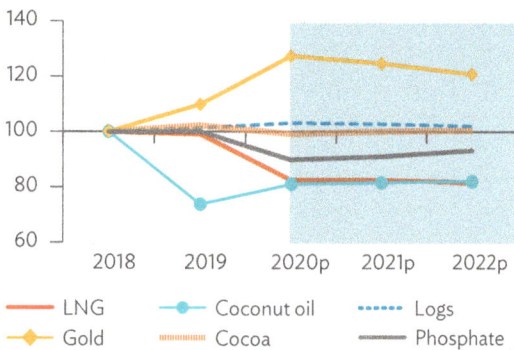

LNG = liquefied natural gas, p = projection.
Source: Asian Development Bank calculations using data from World Bank Commodity Price Data (Pink Sheets).

Tourist Departures to Pacific Destinations
('000 persons, January–April totals)

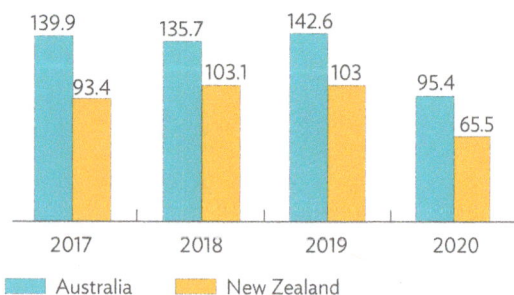

Sources: Australian Bureau of Statistics and Statistics New Zealand.

Lead authors: Noel Del Castillo and Rommel Rabanal.

and border closure, are expected to result in a negative growth of 6.7% in 2020. Robust commodity exports and expectations of stronger business investments outside of the mining industry are expected to support a 6.1% recovery in 2021.

- New Zealand's gross domestic product shrank at an annualized rate of 1.6% in the first quarter of 2020, its first quarterly contraction since the 2010 fourth quarter. Negative growth was observed across all sectors with manufacturing down by 2.7%, followed by services dropping 1.1% and primary industries 1.0%. Travel restrictions and the government's decision to place the country on lockdown affected economic activity, although the brunt of the measures will be felt largely in the second quarter of 2020. As in most countries, prospects for New Zealand are gloomy as lockdown measures are seen to have weakened domestic demand and affected the external sector. The economy is expected to contract by 7.2% in 2020 before bouncing back to 5.9% in 2021.

Widespread declines in global commodity prices amid pandemic shock

- Global commodity prices fell as the COVID-19 pandemic weakened demand and disrupted supply chains. The price of Brent crude oil fell by 20.2% in the first quarter of 2020 compared with the same quarter of the previous year. The initial drop in prices arose from growing concerns over the impact of COVID-19 on oil demand in the PRC. Oil prices further dropped as the outbreak became a pandemic and pushed more countries to impose travel restrictions and lockdowns. The full-year forecast for 2020 indicates a 43.0% drop in oil prices before a gradual recovery in the next few years. On the other hand, prices for most agricultural commodities are expected to remain relatively stable in 2020, with increases in the first quarter being largely offset by declines in the latter part of the year, followed by steady growth starting 2021.

- Average prices of natural gas dropped by 15.5% in first quarter of 2020 (y-o-y). Weak demand at the start of the year further declined as economies felt the impact of COVID-19 mitigation measures. Natural gas prices are expected to fall by 17.0% overall in 2020 and decline further in the next few years. Although cocoa prices are up by 13.8% in the first quarter of 2020, weaker global demand is expected to pull down prices by 3.4% over the full year. Amid elevated uncertainty and aggressive monetary easing by major central banks, gold prices are expected to rise by 15.4% this year, and fall after as the global economy stabilizes.

Tourism to the Pacific plummets with global travel restrictions

- In the North Pacific, Palau, with its heavy reliance on tourists from East Asia, experienced adverse impacts from COVID-19 ahead of its peers in the South Pacific. After posting strong growth (34.4%, y-o-y) in January 2020—continuing strong momentum from November to December 2019—visitor arrivals plunged in February (-42.6%) and March (-69.7%) before grinding to a halt by April.

- In the South Pacific, the adverse impacts of COVID-19 on tourism came after the official declaration by the World Health Organization of a pandemic and subsequent global travel restrictions in March 2020. From solid growth in January and February, tourist departures from Australia to Fiji and Vanuatu—the two main destinations for Australian tourists in the South Pacific—fell by 29.2% and 41.2%, respectively, in March. By April, Fiji only received about 80 arrivals from Australia, while Vanuatu recorded none.

- Some recovery in tourism from New Zealand to major South Pacific destinations, particularly the Cook Islands and Vanuatu, was evident in January–February 2020 after last year's across-the-board decline. However, this was also abruptly reversed by travel restrictions come March, followed by minimal arrivals in April. During the period from January to April 2020, Samoa recorded the sharpest decline (41.6%, y-o-y) in arrivals from New Zealand, reflecting further impacts from travel restrictions related to a measles outbreak that preceded COVID-19.

Impacts of COVID-19 on the Cook Islands economy: Charting a path to recovery

Lead authors: Lily Anne Homasi and James Webb

Since 2012, the Cook Islands has had continuous economic growth averaging 4.9% from fiscal year 2012 (FY2012, ended 30 June) to FY2019 (Figure 1). The island nation became the first Pacific island country to graduate into high-income status in July 2019 (Government of the Cook Islands 2019). Tourism has been the main contributor to this success with tourism receipts equivalent to 61.4% of gross domestic product (GDP) in 2019. Visitor arrivals have generally increased at an average of 6.0% from 1999 to 2019. However, the threat of the coronavirus disease (COVID-19) pandemic pushed the Cook Islands to close its borders on 15 March 2020. This caused significant reductions to tourist arrivals, recording only 5,814 visitors between March and June 2020 compared with 54,756 visitors for the same period in 2019 (Government of the Cook Islands 2020e). The containment measures have prevented the spread of the virus from reaching the Cook Islands, but the fallout of the lockdown has been a complete shutdown of the hospitality sector estimated at 1,556 jobs, or 20.9% of the working population (Government of the Cook Islands 2018).

Figure 1: Cook Islands Real GDP Growth
(annual percentage change)

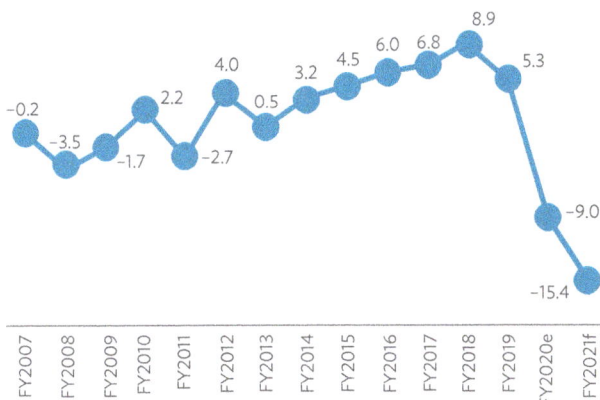

e = estimate, f = forecast, FY = fiscal year, GDP = gross domestic product.
Source: Asian Development Bank estimates.

The Asian Development Bank estimates that GDP will contract by 9.0% in FY2020 and 15.4% in FY2021. These estimates reflect a sharp decline in tourist arrivals from April to June 2020 for FY2020, with this trend extended until December 2020. Unlike the crisis in the 1990s and the global financial crisis in 2008/09, this crisis has impacted multiple sectors of the economy, such as the health, transport, and finance sectors. The crisis in the mid-1990s saw GDP decline by 11.0% between 1996 and 1998, driving a 16.9% decline in the resident population due to emigration to New Zealand (and later, Australia) because of public service cuts. The

2008/09 financial crisis saw a decline of 3.5% of GDP in FY2008. The difference between the mid-1990s and 2008 contractions compared with the present crisis is that the impact of COVID-19 is significantly larger because of the collapse of the tourism sector.

In response to these impacts, the government mobilized NZ$61 million in the first-round stimulus (estimated at 12.2% of GDP in FY2020) and NZ$76 million in the second-round stimulus (estimated at 15.2% of GDP in FY2021). The package included household income support, business support, tax holidays, subsidies to public enterprises, and support to community infrastructure projects. Parallel measures from the public utility waived energy bills for households and discounted bills for businesses. The telecommunication provider extended 50% discounts on services, and banks suspended loan repayments for 6 months.

These responses from the government and the private sector helped mitigate some of the immediate economic damage. However, the underlying challenge of zero tourist arrivals is expected to continue past the August time frame when the government planned to reopen its borders. This necessitates the costly stimulus measures to continue, longer than anticipated, to avoid mass closures of businesses and loss of jobs. With thin private cash reserves and bank liquidity relying on the government and state-owned enterprise cash holdings, this will stretch even the most well-prepared businesses and push public debt levels close to the government's debt ceiling of 35.0% of GDP. Public debt stood at 17.0% of GDP in FY2019, but the policy measures put in by the government will increase debt to 34.8% of GDP by FY2021. The debt position could increase further should the crisis worsen, with the decline in revenue threatening to exhaust cash reserves by late-2021, even with increases in development partner financing (Government of the Cook Islands 2020a).

In terms of immediate policy priorities, efforts to regain tourism market access are at the center of government policy discussions, particularly with New Zealand—the major tourism source market. Since the Cook Islands declared itself COVID-19 free in April 2020 (Government of the Cook Islands 2020d), the government has had discussions with the Government of New Zealand to be included in the New Zealand "travel bubble". While there has been some movement here, no date for open travel has been set. Some of the likely requirements range from ensuring proper airport facilities to cater to the *new normal*, health facilities and supplies, training of essential workers, testing capacity, the ability to contact trace, as well as other standards yet to be determined. These may require additional financing and technical support to complement current institutional capacity. Not carefully managing the health risks could also negatively impact the thin capacity in the Cook Islands to respond to a domestic outbreak. Yet the economic rationale is clear: each month of no visitors arriving into the Cook Islands costs the economy about 3 percentage points in lost GDP and causes significant economic and social damage. The government has implemented a broad range of measures to support economic livelihoods, with many measures extending well beyond the assumed resumption of travel. In the coming months, it is crucial that authorities continue to evaluate and adjust public spending measures to ensure the most effective use of current fiscal reserves. Any improvement in the targeting of support measures would likely create space for continued government interventions if the recovery is slower than expected, and reduce the pressure on accumulated fiscal buffers in the coming months. If travel to the Cook Islands does not resume by December 2020, the fiscal position becomes dire, with development partner support and government reserves likely to run out in the latter half of 2021. Ongoing development partner support may delay the need for drastic fiscal measures, but in either case, a fiscal consolidation in 2021 and beyond will present a significant barrier to future growth.

Beyond the immediate crisis, the Cook Islands continues to face other challenges because of its geography, distance from markets, and low population leading to high costs of doing business. Infrastructure gaps persist as government rebalances immediate and medium-term infrastructure spending to sustain the economy. To this end, there is an opportunity for policymakers and practitioners to reassess the Cook Islands' risk framework to explore ways and sectors that could help to generate other income streams. These could support indirectly the tourism sector. Focusing efforts on low-cost reforms to the regulatory environment that have stalled in recent years is a viable policy option. Examples could include improvements in public sector management, investment policy, immigration, land registry, banking integration with New Zealand, and the delivery of e-Government. Other reforms in the short to medium term could include revisiting its revenue strategy to explore additional gains from the fishery sector and ensure better utilization of the island nation's exclusive economic zone, which spans 1.9 million square kilometers. These efforts, if supported with targeted technical assistance from development partners, could better position the Cook Islands for long-term growth once arrivals resume and mitigate short-term downside risks. Further, the Cook Islands' initiative of a sovereign wealth fund outlined in its 2020/21 budget should capture potential mining and other new revenues, which would eventually reduce government dependency on development partner financing and tourism-driven revenues. Given the dire economic situation, the Cook Islands could draw on lessons from other sovereign wealth funds in the Pacific—the Revenue Equalization Reserve Fund of Kiribati and the Tuvalu Trust Fund—as well as many global examples, to support its efforts with this initiative and minimize extended delays. These immediate, medium-to long-term reforms and initiatives will require collaboration between the government, community, the private sector, and development partners.

Despite robust growth over the last decade, the economy of the Cook Islands has been severely impacted by COVID-19. Although the measures supported through the stimulus package helped

the immediate priorities, there is room for the Cook Islands to explore its macroeconomic risk framework and further improve the targeting of current response measures to extend fiscal resources. Targeted assessment to devise mechanisms to curb and safeguard the Cook Islands from the current and future shocks should align with efforts to ensure fiscal sustainability, stronger institutions, better banking, and deeper private sector engagement, which are all important elements for long-term growth.

References

Asian Development Bank. 2020a. *Asian Development Outlook 2020: What Drives Innovation in Asia? Special Topic: The Impact of the Coronavirus Outbreak – An Update.* Manila.

Asian Development Bank. 2020b. *Asian Development Outlook Supplement: Lockdown, Loosening, and Asia's Growth Prospects.* Manila.

Government of the Cook Islands. 2018. *Cook Islands Population Census 2016 Report.* http://www.mfem.gov.ck/images/documents/ Statistics_Docs/5.Census-Surveys/6.Population-and -Dwelling_2016/2016_CENSUS_REPORT-FINAL.pdf.

Government of the Cook Islands. 2019. *Press Release: Cook Islands Graduation from Official Development Assistance.* http://www .mfem.gov.ck/news1/121-finacial-secretary-officenews/799-press -release-cook-islands-graduation-from-officialdevelopment -assistance.

Government of the Cook Islands. 2020a. *Budget Estimates 2020/21.* http://www.mfem.gov.ck/images/MFEM_Documents/Budget _Books/2020-21/2020-2024_Budget_Book_1_-_Estimates _-_Final.pdf.

Government of the Cook Islands. 2020b. *Economic Response Plan Phase I.* http://www.mfem.gov.ck/economic-planning/covid-19 -erp-phase-1.

Government of the Cook Islands. 2020c. *Economic Response Plan Phase II.* http://www.mfem.gov.ck/economic-planning/erpphase-ii.

Government of the Cook Islands. 2020d. *Press Release: Cook Islands Declared a "COVID-19 Free Zone".* Rarotonga. https://cookislands .travel/news/cook-islands-declared-covid-19-free-zone (accessed 25 June 2020).

Government of the Cook Islands. 2020e. *Tourism and Migration Statistics –March 2020.* http://www.mfem.gov.ck/statistics/social -statistics/tourism-and-migration.

COVID-19 and the Fiji economy: An opportunity to reorient public spending

Lead author: Isoa Wainiqolo

Fiji, like other Pacific island economies, is prone to climatic events. The cost has been substantial at times, with Tropical Cyclone Winston costing almost a fifth of national income (Table 1). While the government tried to make provisions ahead of time by allocating contingency funds for disaster risk, Tropical Cyclone Winston showed that these efforts may not be enough for certain disasters, thus forcing a reprioritization of planned capital outlays. Nishizawa et al. (2019) estimate that, on average, a severe disaster is likely to increase government expenditure by 13.8%–20.6% of gross domestic product (GDP) in the Pacific over a 3-year period.

Table 1: Fiji Selected Disasters

	TC Evan	TC Winston[a]	TC Harold
Time of event	December 2012	February 2016	April 2020
Tropical cyclone (TC) category	4	5	4
Total damage and loss ($ million)	108.9	950.1	46.3
Total damage and loss (% of GDP)	2.5	19.3	0.9

GDP = gross domestic product.
Note: Government figures are for fiscal years ending July 31.
[a] Excludes environmental costs. If environmental costs are included, the loss would equate to almost 28% of GDP.
Source: Government of Fiji.

However, recovery after disasters has been quick (Figure 2). Visitor arrivals were only marginally affected in 2013, while they continued to grow in 2016. COVID-19 presents a much bigger challenge.

Figure 2: Fiji Visitor Arrivals: Post-Disaster Recovery Comparisons

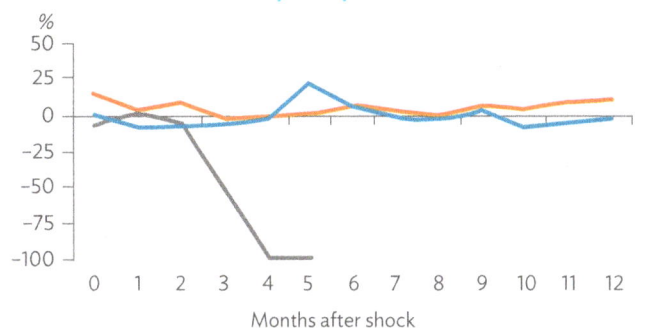

COVID-19 = coronavirus disease, TC = tropical cyclone.
Notes: Series starts in the month that precedes the shock and covers 12 months after. Month 0 = month before the shock. For COVID-19 impact, month 0 refers to December 2019.
Sources: Government of Fiji, Bureau of Statistics; and author's calculations.

The Fiji economy is projected to record an historic economic contraction of 15% in 2020 because of COVID-19.[1] While the handling of the first wave of the pandemic capped the number of cases to 18, with full recovery by early June 2020[2] (Figure 3), the economic fallout from the global travel shutdown has led to massive unemployment and business

Figure 3: Fiji's Road to COVID-19 Containment

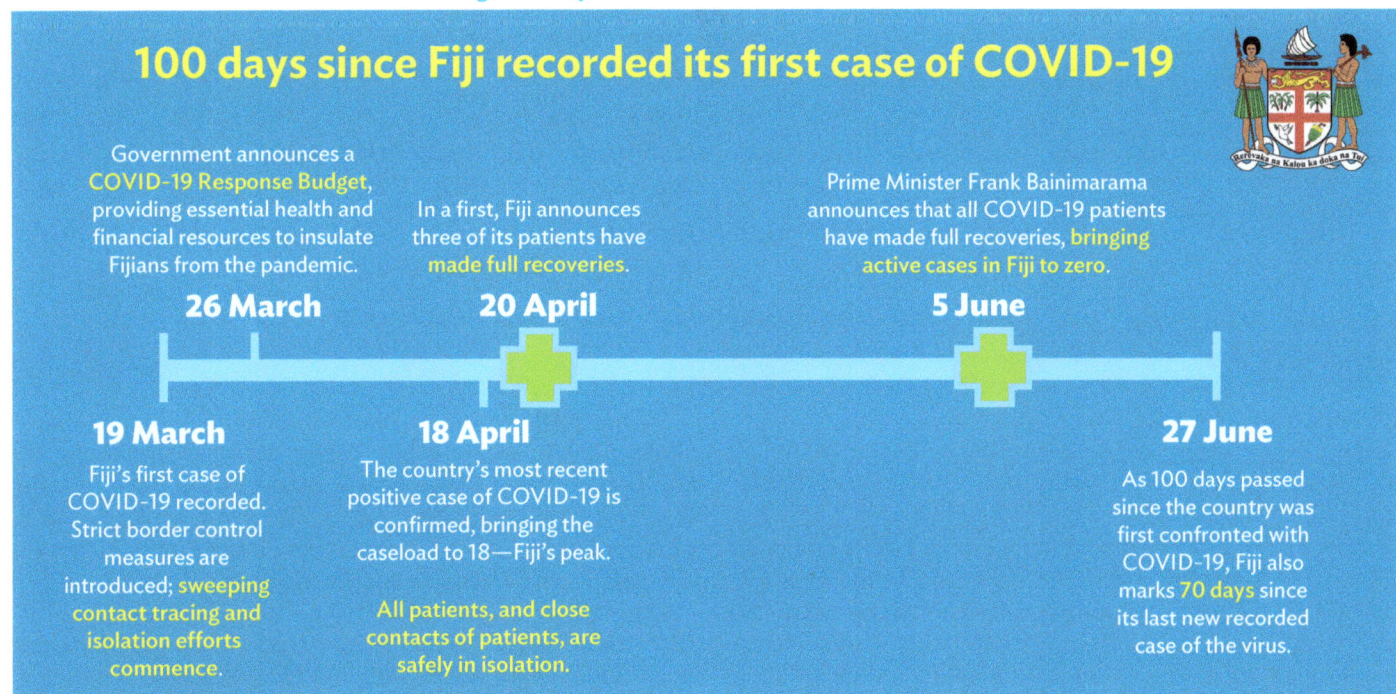

100 days since Fiji recorded its first case of COVID-19

Government announces a **COVID-19 Response Budget,** providing essential health and financial resources to insulate Fijians from the pandemic.
26 March

In a first, Fiji announces three of its patients have **made full recoveries.**
20 April

Prime Minister Frank Bainimarama announces that all COVID-19 patients have made full recoveries, **bringing active cases in Fiji to zero.**
5 June

19 March
Fiji's first case of COVID-19 recorded. Strict border control measures are introduced; **sweeping contact tracing and isolation efforts commence.**

18 April
The country's most recent positive case of COVID-19 is confirmed, bringing the caseload to 18—Fiji's peak.
All patients, and close contacts of patients, are safely in isolation.

27 June
As 100 days passed since the country was first confronted with COVID-19, Fiji also marks **70 days** since its last new recorded case of the virus.

COVID-19 = coronavirus disease.
Note: Fiji recorded a total of 9 new border quarantine cases from 6 July to 21 July, but these are not seen to pose any community transmission risk at this stage.
Source: Government of Fiji, Ministry of Health and Medical Services.

closures. The unemployment rate is projected to increase dramatically.[3] A July 2020 IFC survey, conducted in collaboration with the Government of Fiji (survey period: April 28 to May15 2020 with 3,596 responses), shows that 50% of the tourism businesses surveyed are hibernating or fully closed while 35% are active but with reduced workforce. If the situation does not improve in the next 6 months, around 29% of tourism businesses and 11% of non-tourism businesses expect to go bankrupt.

The impact of the pandemic on the tourism industry and its related sectors is projected to result in negative 16 percentage points to GDP in 2020 (Figure 4). However, the value addition from health sector spending during this period, a result of the vigorous health check campaigns during the lockdown period, and increased activity in the information and communication sector are projected to add 1 percentage point to GDP. The economic damage is expected to continue into 2021, and the tourism industry is projected to return to pre-COVID-19 levels only by 2023,[4] provided a vaccine is identified or borders reopened this year. This is a stark contrast to an economic expansion of 2.5% in 2020 that was projected by the ADB prior to the pandemic.

Figure 4: Fiji Supply-Side Contribution to Growth

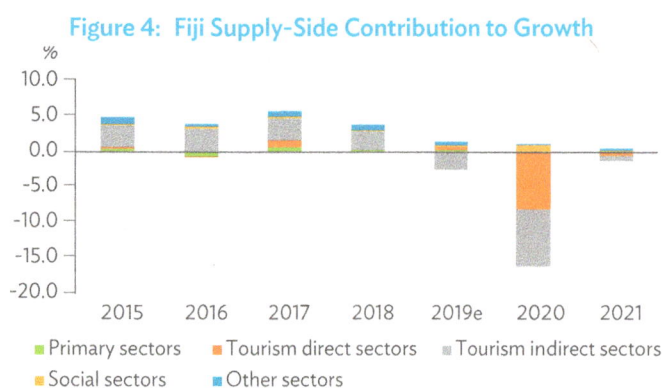

e = estimate, f = forecast.
Note: Primary sectors: agriculture, forestry and logging, fishery and aquaculture, mining and quarrying. Tourism direct sectors: wholesale and retail trade and repair of motor vehicles and motorcycles, transport and storage, accommodation and food service categories. Tourism indirect sectors/line: net taxes, manufacturing, construction, finance and insurance activities, public administration and defense. Social sectors: health, education.
Sources: Government of Fiji, Bureau of Statistics; and author's calculations.

In response, the government announced a supplementary budget of $460 million on 27 March 2020. The budget aims to contain the virus and support low-income households, businesses, and workers affected by the pandemic.

AN OPPORTUNITY TO REORIENT PUBLIC SPENDING

Because of COVID-19, the fiscal deficit is expected to increase to the equivalent of 8.2% of GDP in FY2020 (ends 31 July) compared with the 2.7% of GDP deficit anticipated in July 2019, led by a significant contraction in revenues (Table 2). It will be difficult to counter the decline in value-added tax, which represented 25.0% of total revenue in FY2019 and is estimated to be 33.2% lower than initial budget projections given the lack of tourism activity, high unemployment, and subdued consumer demand. In addition, receipts from customs duties, which accounted for a

further 21% of revenues in FY2019, depend on price and volume variables; and the benign global price environment and supply setbacks will also lead to significant declines. The Government of Fiji recently announced its FY2020-2021 National Budget on 17 July 2020. The F$3.7 billion stimulus budget is expected to generate a net deficit of 20.2% of GDP, pushing debt further to the equivalent of 83.4% of GDP. The higher fiscal deficit is mainly on account of lower revenues due to lower rates on taxes, customs, and excise duties on a broad range of items. Public debt will likely increase to the equivalent of 65.6% of GDP in FY2020 from 49.3% et the end of FY2019 – a significant increase on the 47.1% estimated in the initial FY2020 budget.

In its December 2019 Article IV report, the International Monetary Fund (IMF) suggested that the government pursue growth-friendly fiscal consolidation reforms by cutting back on current spending, which has increased rapidly in 2010-2018 (IMF 2020, p. 6), while revenue collection has potentially reached its peak. The report recommends that current spending be capped at its current real level over the next 5 years; and capital spending at about 10% of GDP, which should include an increased allocation for disaster resiliency (IMF, 2020, p. 6). The government was already on a fiscal consolidation path before COVID-19. Its efforts were complemented by a Public Expenditure Review conducted by the World Bank and a Public Expenditure and Financial Accountability assessment by the IMF.

Table 2: Fiji 2019–2020 Fiscal Framework
(F$ million)

	2018–2019 Actual (A)	2019–2020 Initial Budget (B)	2019–2020 Revised Budget (C)	2020–2021 Budget (D)	% Change (C/B)	% Change (D/C)
Revenue	3,181.1	3,491.7	2,507.6	1,673.6	(28.2)	(33.3)
o/w Tax revenue	2,819.8	3,080.2	2,189.3	1,465.7	(28.9)	(33.1)
o/w Value-added tax	799.6	855.5	571.1	524.3	(33.2)	(8.2)
Customs duties	669.8	746.0	530.4	295.9	(28.9)	(44.2)
Expenditure	3,600.3	3,840.9	3,536.4	3,674.6	(7.9)	3.9
Net deficit	(419.2)	(349.2)	(837.2)	(2,001.0)	139.7	139.0
As a % of GDP	(3.6)	(2.7)	(8.2)	(20.2)		

( ) = negative, GDP = gross domestic product, o/w = of which.
Sources: Government of Fiji, Supplement to the FY2020-2021 Budget Address; budget estimates; and staff calculations.

COVID-19 presents a sizable interim challenge to such consolidation efforts. With the government likely to review its expenditure patterns, this represents an opportunity to reorient public spending during and after the pandemic. Fiji would be well-placed to focus on increasing the quality of public spending and returns on the public tax dollar. Fiscal buffers will need to be rebuilt to mitigate the future risks of climate change.

To limit the budget deficit in this *new normal*, possible consideration would be to allow for more effective targeting of expenditure programs, with defined objectives and deliverables. Areas that do not meet the agreed criterion can be postponed, reprogrammed, or eliminated from public spending. In the short term, however, the need for fiscal stimulus persists.

The government could focus on targeted fiscal stimulus that lowers the overall cost of the intervention, but maximizes the economic and social benefits. This may delay the need for additional, significant debt financing in advance of borders reopening and the resumption of tourism. Coming out of this crisis, Fiji cannot afford to rely on fiscal stimulus as its primary economic tool and must realign spending to allow the accumulation of fiscal buffers. Failure to do this will result in worsening fiscal balances and a missed opportunity to cut back on unproductive spending.

Endnotes

[1]   In its latest assessment released on 2 July 2020, the Government of Fiji's estimate now projects a 21.7% contraction for 2020, a significant downgrade from the 4.3% contraction it announced in March 2020. In addition, it estimates a 1.3% contraction for 2019. However, the official provisional estimate for 2019 will be released on or before the last quarter of 2020 by the Fiji Bureau of Statistics. The government projects a 14.1% recovery in 2021.

[2]   While Fiji managed to contain COVID-19, 9 new border quarantine cases were identified in July 2020. However, they do not pose any community transmission risk at this stage.

[3]   Fiji Airways laid off 775 staff, Air Terminal Services 285 staff, and Sofitel Hotel 166 staff; and InterContinental Fiji Golf Resort & Spa will make redundant 483 workers. The Fiji Hotel and Tourism Association estimates that, at the height of the lockdown, about 86,000 were affected and on various forms of reduced employment. The International Labour Organization estimated that a total of 115,000 workers were affected. This equates to 32.2% of the 2017 census of the labor force. Sources: Various media reports.

[4]   In line with the International Air Transport Association's projection on global travel.

References

International Monetary Fund. 2020. 2019 *Article IV Consultation Staff Report*. Washington, DC.

Nishizawa, H., S. Roger, and H. Zhang. 2019. *Fiscal Buffers for Natural Disasters in Pacific Island Countries*. IMF Working Paper 19/152. https://www.imf.org/en/Publications/WP/Issues/2019/07/12/Fiscal-Buffers-for-Natural-Disasters-in-Pacific-Island-Countries-47011

Remoteness redux: COVID-19 impacts in the Federated States of Micronesia and the Marshall Islands

Lead authors: Cara Tinio and Rommel Rabanal

Like many Pacific countries, the Federated States of Micronesia (FSM) and the Marshall Islands have managed to stay free of COVID-19. Mindful of the serious implications an outbreak would have on their health care systems, both countries were quick to close their borders to inbound travelers to avoid the importation of the virus.

Nevertheless, the FSM and the Marshall Islands remain linked to the global economy and would still feel the impacts from the pandemic. Recent studies by ADB explore the economic impacts on its developing member countries through the following channels:

(i)   trade and tourism flows, which are constrained by border controls, travel restrictions, and reduced air and sea operations that would reduce remittances from overseas workers employed in related sectors and earnings for tourism-related sectors, as well as raise costs of traded goods;

(ii)   local productivity and consumption, which can be dampened by domestic mobility restrictions (e.g., lockdowns and similar community quarantine measures, voluntary social distancing, and sheltering at home) that further limit the movement of inputs to production as well as end purchases of goods and services; and

(iii)   government spending, which would help support businesses and households through their economic difficulties caused by the pandemic.

This article examines the impacts of the COVID-19 pandemic on growth prospects in the FSM and the Marshall Islands for FY2020 and FY2021 (ends 30 September for both economies). It discusses the way the pandemic is seen to affect the channels mentioned. However, given the rapidly evolving nature of government responses, this article does not discuss these measures or their economic impacts in detail.

FEDERATED STATES OF MICRONESIA

As early as January, the FSM declared a health emergency and imposed restrictions on both domestic and international travelers from COVID-19-affected locations. This was followed by full border closures across all four states by March. The state and national governments each have developed respective COVID-19 action plans and are implementing preparedness measures.

Because of these border closures, the COVID-19 pandemic is seen to affect the FSM economy largely through constraints on trade and travel flows. Advisories and reduced flights would directly depress the performance of the transport sector, particularly transshipment of fish catch from purse seine vessels that now cannot dock at local ports. The Graduate School USA's Pacific Islands Training Initiative estimates transshipment output to fall by more than a third over FY2020–FY2021. Private transshipment operations are seen to fall by 80% during this period; indeed, the private sector is expected to bear the brunt of the overall impact of the pandemic with constrained trade and travel impacting business activities.

Trade and travel restrictions are expected also to constrain small-scale exports of fish and agricultural products, which are transported via air cargo or carried by travelers, and the movement of specialists and imported inputs to private construction projects. Most development partner-funded projects are still in the planning and design stages, so the COVID-19 pandemic should have little effect on these.

Further, although tourism is not a large component of the FSM economy, pandemic-related constraints are seen to bring about a significant drop-off in visitors. International controls and reduced air operations are expected to limit foreign visitors, while state-level travel controls are seen to reduce overall public mobility. These combined effects are likely to dampen wholesale and retail trade activity, with aviation fuel sales expected to drop by 85% in FY2020–FY2021.

Providing a bright spot to the outlook are domestic commercial fishing and fishing support services, which are expected to be largely unaffected by the pandemic. Fishing output is even seen to increase, though this is largely because of the base effects of a weak performance in FY2019. Earnings from fishing license fees under the vessel day scheme of the Parties to the Nauru Agreement, a major source of government revenues, are seen to remain steady in FY2020–FY2021 with the FSM having sold all of its allocated vessel days for 2020 and with skipjack tuna prices seen to rise next year; however, continued travel and trade restrictions affecting fisheries operations may reduce future demand, as well as the going rate, for vessel days in the near-term.

Trade and mobility constraints are also expected to alter government spending patterns, with budgets unused under the pandemic (e.g., for official travel, utilities) reallocated to areas where more resources are needed. However, total expenditure requirements are seen to spike in the near-term, with an additional $26 million for health systems strengthening along with government's $15 million economic stimulus package and $1 million for tourism sector support. High revenue inflows in the past years—from a FY2019 spike in taxes on foreign corporations using the FSM domicile, as well as from fishing license revenues—have allowed the national government to build reserves (outside of deposits into the FSM Trust Fund) and provided some fiscal breathing room despite reduced domicile tax receipts. Nonetheless, while available resources including external grants appear enough to cover FY2020 needs, a large financing gap is likely in FY2021 (Figure 5), requiring further assistance from the FSM's development partners to avoid depletion of fiscal buffers or contractionary fiscal policy that can exacerbate the economic downturn further. Fiscal strain is heightened further at the state level, where governments largely depend on transfers under the FSM's Compact of Free Association with the United States.

Figure 5: A large FY2021 financing gap is likely in the Federated States of Micronesia.
(Federated States of Micronesia fiscal outcomes, % of GDP)

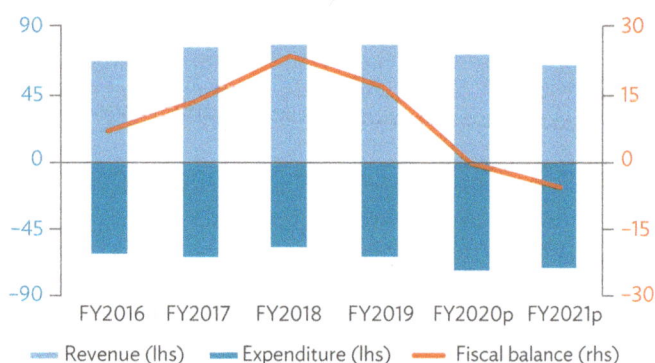

FY = fiscal year, GDP = gross domestic product, lhs = left-hand scale, p = projection, rhs = right-hand scale.
Sources: EconMAP. 2019. Federated States of Micronesia Fiscal Year 2018 Economic Review and Asian Development Bank estimates.

The FSM economy is projected to contract by 2.0% in FY2020, and again by 1.5% in FY2021. These forecasts already consider the possible impacts of government efforts to stimulate domestic demand. The Graduate School USA estimates that the COVID-19 pandemic would eliminate the equivalent of 1,841 full-time jobs over FY2020–FY2021, an 11% drop from FY2019 levels. The impacts are seen to be greatest in the transport and hotel and restaurant sectors, which account for almost 70% of the jobs lost, and would be felt mostly by the private sector.

MARSHALL ISLANDS

The Marshall Islands began implementing travel and shipping restrictions in late January 2020 and declared a state of health emergency because of COVID-19 on 7 February. The government announced a preparedness and response plan. As of this writing, bans on incoming travelers and domestic travel via international carriers remain in effect, and implementation of preparedness measures continues.

The impacts of the pandemic on the economy of the Marshall Islands also come mainly through constraints on trade and travel flows, with the fisheries sector taking most of the hit. Flight suspensions are already contributing to the drop in the exports of aquarium fish, and 14-day quarantine requirements still in place for fishing vessels are seen to affect related on-shore services (e.g., tuna loining, net repair, transshipment of fish catch).

Trade and travel constraints will hit also the Marshall Islands' small hotel and restaurant sector, with restaurants depending on visitors for more than 50% of their business, and construction. Although development partner-funded projects appear on track for FY2020, a decline is expected in FY2021 because of project completion as well as implementation constraints related to limited mobility of specialists (although some can work remotely) and access to equipment and materials. The recent easing of quarantine requirements for eligible cargo vessels and fuel tankers may reduce some of the pandemic's expected negative impacts in this respect.

Further, COVID-19 is limiting mobility within the country. Although there have been no local lockdowns similar to countries that are hosting confirmed cases, schools have revised their calendars and public events have been either cancelled or postponed. Weaker demand from diminished movements and social interaction will negatively impact the wholesale and retail trade sector. In addition, mobility restrictions could limit locals' access to the United States military base on Kwajalein atoll. Although operations currently proceed as normal and are excluded from national accounts, the Marshallese workers employed at the base account for 16% of employee income nationwide. Any significant changes to operations, e.g., through heightened security measures, would affect these workers' jobs and their incomes' impact on their communities.

The Government of the Marshall Islands will need to adjust its operations in FY2020 and F2021 in response to the risks associated with the pandemic and in anticipation of lower revenues. The FY2020 budget reduces transfers to the Marshall Islands Social Security Administration and the country's Compact Trust Fund, offsetting expected lower tax collections and narrowing the fiscal deficit compared with FY2019. Although about 27% of the Marshall Islands' allotted vessel days remain unsold for 2020, the shortfall in fishing license revenues will be compensated for by transfers of reserves from the Marshall Islands Marine Resources Authority, the entity responsible for managing the country's fisheries and participation in the Parties to the Nauru Agreement vessel day scheme. The deficit is seen to widen in the following fiscal year with tax collections remaining weak, fishing license revenues declining on anticipated lower vessel day rates, and added fiscal pressure to provide social safety nets and business support for those affected by the pandemic. The absence of any policy adjustment to government expenditures, e.g., maintaining unsustainably high levels of subsidies to state-owned enterprises, will also contribute to the heightened pressure on fiscal resources amid limited reserves and financing options.

The economy of the Marshall Islands is expected to contract by 5.5% in FY2020, a decline comparable with the one experienced during the 2008–2009 global financial and economic crisis (Figure 6), and further by 1.4% in FY2021. With government operations expected to continue as planned, the private sector would feel most of the adverse economic impacts from the COVID-19 pandemic. Employment loss in FY2020–F2021 is estimated to be equivalent to 716 full-time jobs, almost three quarters of which would be in the transport, trade, and hotel and restaurant sectors. Jobs are expected to be created and lost in the construction sector, tracking the progress of project implementation during the period, while jobs would be lost and subsequently created in the tuna loining operation, following the effect of pandemic-related trade and travel restrictions on the fisheries and transport sectors.

Figure 6: The projected contraction for the Marshall Islands economy is comparable with the one experienced during the 2008-2009 global economic and financial crisis.
(real GDP growth, %)

FY = fiscal year, GDP = gross domestic product, p = projection.
Sources: Asian Development Outlook 2020 database and Asian Development Bank estimates.

Conclusion and recommendations

That the COVID-19 pandemic's impacts would be mainly through constraints on trade and travel is not surprising, considering that both the economies of the FSM and the Marshall Islands depend on imported inputs and linkages to global transport networks. Local mobility restrictions are affecting these economies to a lesser extent because of the small share of tourism and travel in gross domestic product, and absence of strict lockdown measures that would otherwise radically disrupt citizens' daily lives.

Policy responses must, thus, strike a balance between heading off the economic downturn expected from the COVID-19 pandemic and avoiding severe deterioration of fiscal sustainability. Managing expenditures becomes even more necessary, given the added demands of emergency response and risk mitigation. The Marshall Islands would need to rationalize subsidies, which will pose a sizable fiscal burden not just in the current situation but also later when Compact grants are no longer available. Also, both the FSM and the Marshall Islands should use this opportunity to implement high return public investment projects when resources, notably labor, are less scarce. Further, any COVID-19 assistance or relief measures, including tax deferments, must be carefully targeted to mitigate the impacts of the pandemic while encouraging the efficient use of resources.

For their part, development partners are stepping up assistance for these economies. ADB has expanded the coverage of its disaster resilience financing to include health-related emergencies, providing quick-disbursing financing to certain Pacific developing member countries including the FSM and the Marshall Islands, and is working to make added resources available under its COVID-19 Pandemic Response Option modality. These increased resources should help bolster health care systems and soften the pandemic's socioeconomic impacts. Trade and travel restrictions must now be taken into account in designing new projects and added support, including capacity building, in project management and implementation would help the governments make the most of their resource envelope. Coordination among development partners, and between development partners and beneficiary governments, remains crucial to avoid redundant interventions. Well-coordinated and well-implemented responses would help the FSM and the Marshall Islands to weather the pandemic without sacrificing any progress in addressing longer-term development challenges.

References

The Marshall Islands Journal. 2020. RMI Extends Travel Ban. 11 June. https://marshallislandsjournal.com/rmi-extends-travel-ban/

C. Park et al. 2020. An Updated Assessment of the Economic Impact of COVID-19. *ADB Briefs.* No. 133. Manila: ADB.

Graduate School USA. 2020. *Assessing the Impact of COVID-19 on the Marshall Islands Economy.* https://pitiviti.org/news/downloads/RMI_EconFiscalImpact_COVID-19_May2020_Web.pdf.

Graduate School USA. 2020. *Assessing the Impact of COVID-19 on the Federated States of Micronesia Economy.* https://pitiviti.org/news/downloads/FSM_EconImpact_COVID-19_June2020_Web.pdf.

Connell, J. et al. 2019. Managing unconventional revenue streams. *Pacific Economic Monitor.* Manila: ADB (December).

Impact of COVID-19 on small economies—Kiribati and Tuvalu: Recasting essential reforms

Lead authors: Lily Anne Homasi and Isoa Wainiqolo

Kiribati and Tuvalu are two of the few countries in the world without any reported COVID-19 cases. Their remoteness and their governments' prompt decisions to close their ports of entry have insulated them from the pandemic. However, some impact from these border closures is expected to be felt because they rely heavily on public spending and external funding to drive economic activity. This article highlights the economic and social impact of the COVID-19 pandemic, as well as the measures put in place by governments to mitigate risks, and explores opportunities for recovery.

ADB estimates that the economic growth of Kiribati in 2020 will slow to 0.6% and Tuvalu to 2.0%, compared with average growth rates of over 4% for both countries for the period 2015–2019 (ADB 2020b) (Figure 7). The brunt of the impact is expected to come through the construction, remittances, and export channels. Restrictions on the movement of labor and capital equipment have delayed infrastructure projects and led to the loss of income from jobs in the construction and hospitality sectors. Seafarers and seasonal workers have been also impacted because of challenges in cross-border mobilization, and business inventories have been disrupted because of supply chain bottlenecks. For instance, the Government of Kiribati estimates about 1,040 persons (3.7% of Kiribati's 28,158 working population) to lose their jobs or become temporarily unemployed because of COVID-19 impacts (Government of Kiribati 2015, 2020). Of this, 69% of job losses came from the domestic market and 31% offshore. I-Kiribati impacted include 277 seafarers and fisheries observers, 46 seasonal workers/fruit pickers, 577 employed by private businesses and state-owned enterprises, and 140 workers from the tourism sector.

Financial market volatility also affected these countries' sovereign wealth funds—the Revenue Equalization Reserve Fund of Kiribati and the Tuvalu Trust Fund. The COVID-19 effects on financial markets drove down the Revenue Equalization Reserve Fund's value by A$52.4 million, or 4.6% of the A$1.14 billion fund (Government of Kiribati 2020) in March 2020. From April, the markets improved where the Dow Jones has grown by about 30%, a positive development. However, uncertainty remains for the remainder of 2020 and for 2021 because of the pandemic's influence on geopolitical factors and investor confidence in the financial markets. Given the importance of these funds in supplementing budget priorities, it is critical to monitor COVID-19 impacts on these funds.

Moreover, Kiribati and Tuvalu also anticipate declines in revenue. In Tuvalu, receipts from value-added tax, company tax, excise tax, and room tax are projected to fall. In Kiribati, the government expects a 5%–10% fall in fishing revenues in 2020 compared with 2019 because of delays in transshipments and the limited number of observers on fishing vessels to monitor and account for the catches. On the other hand, Tuvalu expects minimal impact on fishing license revenues because of the small number of vessels that delayed entry into Funafuti for transshipment transshipment (Government of Tuvalu 2020a). However, downside risks include a worsening pandemic resulting in the closure of canneries in Thailand, the Philippines, and the Republic of Korea—the main markets for tuna—leading to lower demand for vessel days (Government of Tuvalu, 2020c). The pandemic has also reduced remittances, which accounts for 10% and 8% of gross domestic product (GDP) in both Kiribati and Tuvalu, respectively (World Bank 2020).

Further, Kiribati and Tuvalu have been often associated with weak health outcomes as reflected in mortality rates and noncommunicable diseases (NCD). The World Health Organization identifies old age and medical conditions related to pre-existing NCDs as high-risk factors for COVID-19, both of which are prevalent in Kiribati and Tuvalu (Table 1, page 27). According to the Tuvalu 2017 census, about 10% of the populace is aged 60 years and above. The small island economy is among the top ten countries in the world for the prevalence of diabetes in 20–79 age group (World Bank, 2020). According to the Government of Tuvalu's 2018 review of its medical scheme, 35% of patients who were referred for overseas treatment are aged 55 years and above and have pre-existing medical conditions. Since 2017, spending on the Tuvalu Medical Treatment Scheme has exceeded the government's fiscal target of 6% of domestic revenue. The government expects the costs of the health tertiary scheme to continue increasing over time. Political influence and capacity constraints at the local hospitals are adding pressure to costly scheme and, in turn, to future fiscal resources. In Kiribati, life expectancy and infant mortality rates are unfavorable compared with its regional neighbors. Issues such as inadequate water and sanitation facilities, poor nutrition, smoking, and limited housing options all contribute to these health risks. Kiribati has the highest prevalence of tuberculosis in the Pacific. NCDs have grown from an estimated 38.8% of the disease burden in 1900 to 58.1% in 2015 (World Bank 2018). Cerebrovascular diseases, diabetes, and ischemic heart disease were responsible for the largest shares of the overall disease burden. The limited health facilities, equipment, and personnel; and inadequate water and sanitation facilities could exacerbate the bleak situation should COVID-19 reach Kiribati and Tuvalu.

Figure 7: Kiribati and Tuvalu Real GDP Growth

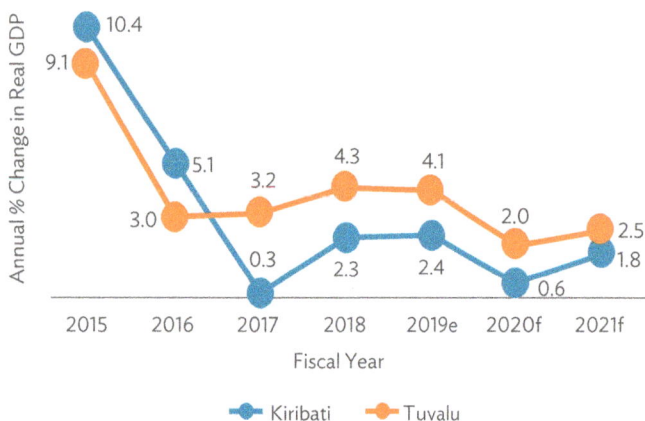

e = estimate, f = forecast, GDP = gross domestic product.
Source: Asian Development Bank estimates.

To mitigate these risks, these countries implemented COVID-19 plans that focus on preparedness, response, and recovery.

In March 2020, the Government of Tuvalu passed a 2020 Supplementary Budget worth A$18.9 million (31.0% of GDP in 2019), which includes allocations for essential medical equipment and emergency response programs; allocations for chartered flights to bring medical equipment and supplies, including citizens, back to Tuvalu; renovation of isolation wards to accommodate suspected cases; salaries of Tuvaluans and expatriate doctors; maintenance of quarantine centers to accommodate those who need to undergo the mandatory 14-day quarantine; and a working capital facility to assist the private sector in acquiring sufficient basic food items (Government of Tuvalu, 2020a). This economic relief package is part of the government's national worse-case scenario plan (*Talaaliki Plan*).

Meanwhile, the Government of Kiribati mobilized its COVID-19 preparedness and response plan in June, valued at A$32.9 million (12.5% of GDP in 2019). The bulk of the funding will be for social and financial support (37.2%), health preparedness (36.2%), food security (12.4%), and education (9.2%). The remaining funds will support transportation, public awareness campaign, and small infrastructure works to refurbish isolation centers. Grants and subsidies are expected to be provided to businesses as well as state-owned enterprises to continue basic support services to the public. There will also be grants for unemployed I-Kiribati impacted by COVID-19, including seafarers, fisheries observers, fruit pickers, and casual workers in the construction and tourism industries.

Beyond these efforts, the pandemic highlighted limitations in some areas of public service provision. For instance, inefficient procurement practices delay the provision of medical equipment and supplies. Also, the high incidence of NCDs, low health system capacity (even prior to COVID 19), and high spending—with a third of health budgets spent on tertiary medical treatment schemes—are risks and limitations that are important to be addressed. With borders closed, there is an opportunity for policymakers and practitioners to revisit the primary goal of health care service delivery, and adjust the business plan to implement critical reforms on primary health care as a means of reducing the dependence on costly tertiary health schemes. Inefficiencies in certain areas of public sector management also cause a missed opportunity to better deliver on education, disaster risk management, and public financial management outcomes.

The thin labor market and public sector capacity constraints, which limit the conduct of regular functions as well as management of risks associated with COVID-19, are ongoing issues. These could be supported with targeted technical assistance from development partners to support civil service reforms that would right-size the work force, while potentially creating roles that will help Kiribati and Tuvalu to determine its new ways of working under the *new normal*.

Besides the mechanical governance issues, the distance from markets is a challenge to these island nations' coordination efforts. However, this could also be an opportunity for these nations to regroup and prioritize investments in information and communication technology (ICT) and public sector management. In the short term, policymakers

and practitioners could consider reallocating funds from low-return investments and tapping existing partnerships with development partners to finance low-cost investments that would strengthen the ICT sector and extend the internet bandwidth. Kiribati and Tuvalu could also support tailored public sector reforms to strengthen data management, health, education, disaster management information systems, and public procurement systems which are critical in decision-making. Investments in training and development through implementation of low-cost infrastructure projects will also help position these countries to quickly kick-start major projects once the borders reopen. Securing the services of an advisory group from national, regional, and international experts to guide the way forward will position Kiribati and Tuvalu to lead a steady path to recovery.

To complement the way forward, efforts to increase access to broadband internet connections in Kiribati and Tuvalu are key to making this focus on governance and ICT sector improvements a reality (ADB 2019). ICT support to strengthen public financial management systems as well as e-learning, e-medicine, and e-billing/e-procurement will increase the efficiency and the quality of government services to sustain themselves during COVID-19, as well as position themselves on the road to recovery.

References

Asian Development Bank. 2019. *Asia Pacific: Remote Broadband Internet Satellite Project.* https://www.adb.org/projects/53115-001/main#projectpds.

Asian Development Bank. 2020a. *Asian Development Outlook 2020: What Drives Innovation in Asia? Special Topic: The Impact of the Coronavirus Outbreak – An Update.* Manila.

Asian Development Bank. 2020b. *Asian Development Outlook Supplement: Lockdown, Loosening, and Asia's Growth Prospects.* Manila.

Government of Kiribati. 2015. *National Census.* Tarawa.

Government of Kiribati. 2019. *National Budget.* Tarawa.

Government of Kiribati. 2020. *Kiribati COVID-19 Preparedness and Response Plan.* Tarawa.

Government of Tuvalu. 2020a. *COVID-19 National Financial Relief Package.* Funafuti.

Government of Tuvalu. 2020b. *Taaliki Plan – A comprehensive COVID-19 worst case scenario plan.* Funafuti.

Government of Tuvalu. 2020c. *National Response Budget.* Funafuti.

Secretariat of the Pacific Community. 2020. *The Economic and Social Impacts of the COVID-19: Pandemic on the Pacific Island Economies.* http://sdd.spc.int/news/2020/04/29/economic-and-socialimpact-covid-19-pandemic-pacific-island-economies.

World Bank. 2018. *International Development Association Program Document for a Proposed Development Policy Grant in the Amount of*

SDR 5.2 Million (US$7.5 million equivalent) to Tuvalu for the Fourth Development Policy Operation. http://documents.worldbank.org/curated/en/357821535859034516/pdf/Tuvalu-edited-PAD-08092018.pdf

World Bank. 2018. *Kiribati Health Financing System Assessment: SPEND BETTER.* Washington, DC.

World Bank. 2020. World Development Indicators. https://data.worldbank.org/ (accessed 23 July 2020).

World Health Organization. Q&A: Older people and COVID-19. https://www.who.int/emergencies/diseases/novel-coronavirus-2019/question-and-answers-hub/q-a-detail/q-a-on-on-covid-19-for-older-people.

COVID-19: Compounding the challenges of geographic remoteness in Nauru

Lead authors: Jacqueline Connell and Prince Cruz

As a single island—measuring 21 square kilometers—with one of the highest population densities in the Pacific, Nauru could face severe impacts if COVID-19 would arrive and spread in its communities. Many of its people would be vulnerable because of the high incidence of noncommunicable diseases, which represent a risk factor (CDC 2020). More than 60% of adults and 33% of children in Nauru are obese, the highest in the world, according to the World Health Organization (WHO 2020). Further, more than half of the adult population uses tobacco, twice the global average (Table 1, page 27). The country has limited health facilities with only one hospital. It uses a tertiary referral system with about one-third of the health budget spent on overseas referrals.

The government has taken early and proactive measures to reduce the risk of COVID-19. In January, it imposed restrictions on travelers from a growing list of COVID-19-affected countries. The government declared a state of emergency on 16 March. International arrivals, including citizens, were required to quarantine in a hotel, passenger flights were reduced to once every 2 weeks, and quarantine screening was imposed on air and sea freight.

Nauru's remoteness and the strict containment measures at the border have proved effective in preventing COVID-19 from entering the country. But these have compounded the economic challenges the country already faced because of its small size and distance from markets. Nauru's narrow-based economy is highly dependent on imports, especially for food, fuel, and medical supplies. These rely on global transport networks, which were disrupted by COVID-19. The government reported that sea freight costs have risen in 2020 and the cargo ship that was scheduled to reach Nauru in March was delayed until the end of May, impacting business inventories and retail supplies (Government of Nauru 2020a).

Construction of Nauru's new port, its biggest infrastructure project ever, was also disrupted because it relies on imports of construction materials and foreign workers. This had follow-on impacts to services, Nauru's biggest sector.

Aside from containment measures at the border, businesses, shops, and schools have generally remained open. The public service, which is a large source of employment and aggregate demand, has continued to operate with government expenditure remaining high. This has helped to mitigate the economic impacts of COVID-19 in Nauru. Despite this, the economy is estimated to have contracted by 1.7% in FY2020, ending 30 June 2020, from 1.0% growth in the previous year. Marginal growth of 0.8% is projected for FY2021 (Figure 8).

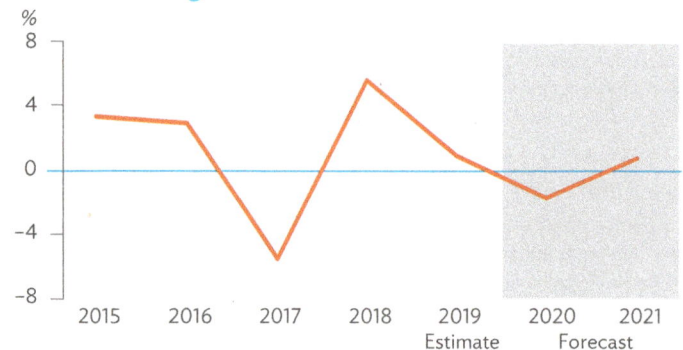

Figure 8: Nauru Economic Growth

Source: Asian Development Bank estimates using data from the International Monetary Fund and Nauru Statistics Bureau.

The government's initial fiscal response to COVID-19 focused on containment measures, health preparedness, and cash flow support to the state-owned Nauru Airlines—the sole carrier servicing the country—to ensure that critical services would be maintained.

Preliminary data for FY2020 indicate that government revenue collections exceeded budget estimates. Revenues from fishing licenses, taxation, and revenues related to the Regional Processing Center for asylum seekers more than offset travel-related income streams that were impacted by COVID-19. A fiscal surplus of about 9.4% of GDP is estimated by the government, including its contributions to the Nauru Trust Fund, which is a long-term investment vehicle intended to provide long-term fiscal financing

Reflecting the impact of COVID-19 on financial markets, the value of investments in the Nauru Trust Fund fell by 4.3% to A$116 million at the end of March 2020, the first annual negative return since its establishment (Government of Nauru 2020a).

The budget for FY2021 is framed against considerable revenue uncertainty (Government of Nauru 2020b). A protracted global slowdown because of COVID-19, or volatile commodity prices, could affect demand for fishing days and licenses in Nauru's waters which supply some 30% of domestic revenue. The future arrangements for the Regional Processing Centre, which accounts for more than half of domestic revenues, remain uncertain after 2020.

The FY2021 budget estimates revenues and expenditures at 15% below the previous year's revised budget (Figure 9). The budget includes A$18.5 million (equal to 10.9% of GDP) to support the government's COVID-19 response. More than half of this is allocated toward mitigating risks to food security and supplies arising because of COVID-19, including additional support to ensure that the national airline continues to provide air services, and a ship charter to improve sea freight links. The remainder of the COVID-19 response financing is allocated toward health preparedness, quarantine, and containment costs in FY2021.

Figure 9: Revenues of the Government of Nauru

% of gross domestic product

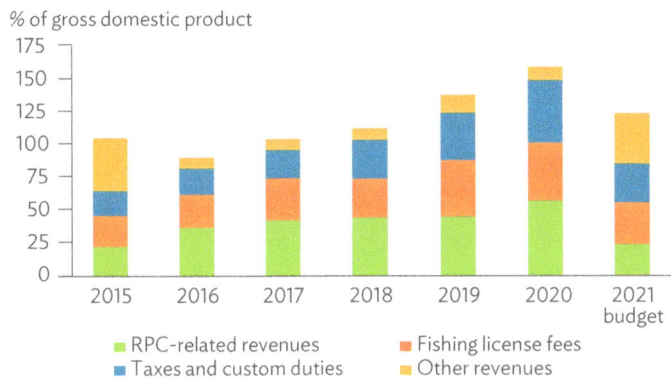

RPC = Regional Processing Center.
Source: Asian Development Bank estimates using data from Nauru budget documents.

The government's revenue collections, along with development partner support, have enabled it to mitigate some of the economic and supply chain impacts of COVID-19. Reducing lower-priority government expenditure will be critical over the medium term when revenues are expected to decline. Continuing to reconcile public debt and strengthen debt management will also improve fiscal sustainability. Equally important is continuing to improve the governance of state-owned enterprises (SOEs). Subsidies to SOEs spiked in FY2020, rising to the equivalent of 20.5% of GDP, including support to Nauru Airlines. The FY 2021 budget reduces subsidies to SOEs and introduces a new community service obligation framework, recognizing that some SOEs are directed to pursue non-commercial, social objectives. To reduce risks to food and supply security because of COVID-19, for example, the government will provide a community service obligation to support the state-owned airline and port authority in maintaining regular air and sea freight services at pre-COVID-19 price levels, despite the operational impacts of the pandemic.

References

Asian Development Bank. 2020. *Asian Development Outlook Supplement: Lockdown, Loosening, and Asia's Growth Prospects.* Manila.

Center for Diseases Control (CDC). 2020. *Coronavirus Disease 2019 (COVID-19): People of Any Age with Underlying Medical Conditions.* https://www.cdc.gov/coronavirus/2019-ncov/need-extra-precautions/people-with-medical-conditions.html.

Government of Nauru. 2020a. *2020–21 Budget and Estimates of Revenues and Expenditures: Budget Paper 1, Budget Strategy and Outlook.* Yaren.

Government of Nauru. 2020b. *2020–21 Budget: Budget Paper 2.* Yaren.

International Monetary Fund. 2020. *Republic of Nauru: 2019 Article IV Consultation-Press Release; Staff Report; and Statement by the Executive Director for the Republic of Nauru.* Washington, DC.

World Health Organization. 2020. *World Health Statistics 2020.* https://www.who.int/gho/publications/world_health_statistics/2020/en/.

Niue: Preparing for a restart in tourism

Lead author: Rommel Rabanal

With a population of only about 1,700 people, the capacity constraints that are common across the Pacific islands are even more acute in Niue. The health system's capacity to respond to any potential cases of COVID-19 is severely limited, with only 5 doctors, 13 nurses, 10 hospital beds, and 1 ventilator currently on-island. Further, Niue's population could face heightened risks of transmission because of the high incidence of co-morbidities, including respiratory diseases, obesity, and diabetes.

To safeguard its population and fragile health system, the government acted proactively to prevent possible importation of the virus. On 23 March 2020, the Niue National Disaster Council activated "Code Yellow" in its alert system—just a step below a state of emergency—signifying an imminent threat that requires response measures to prevent widespread disease transmission. Chief among these measures is a reduction in passenger flights into Niue, from a normal twice-weekly schedule to now only once every 2 weeks. The number of passengers per flight has also been restricted to 26 to ensure social distancing, translating to a maximum monthly arrival of 52 passengers from the usual 1,200. As these flights are only open to returning residents and essential workers, Niue's tourism sector is effectively shut down temporarily.

Outside of the public sector, tourism has been the main driver of economic growth in Niue. Annual arrivals reach about 10,000—more than 5 times the resident population—and tourism receipts are the equivalent of about a third of its annual GDP. During 2013–2018, GDP growth averaged 4.4%, supported by solid tourism performance and a resumption in development partner-supported capital projects later in the period. Although some moderation in the rate of increase in visitor arrivals was experienced in 2019, GDP growth is estimated to have remained positive. However, with inbound tourism likely on hold for at least 6 months, the economy is now expected to contract in 2020.

In its *Economic Response to COVID-19 Briefing Paper*, the government estimates financing needs during April–September 2020 to total $12.9 million or the equivalent of 38.4% of GDP (Figure 10). This covers support across three main areas, including:

- **Health and well-being:** for medical supplies and equipment, frontline health workers, as well as food security

- **Employment and business support:** providing wage subsidies directly to affected workers or through business owners, interest-free loans to businesses, and direct support for Niue's largest tourist resort that currently serves as the only isolation center
- **Core public service:** financing emerging funding gaps amid revenue losses and additional spending requirements, plus support continuing operations of basic utilities

Funding is also allocated for repairs to critical infrastructure damaged by Cyclone Tino in January 2020 and for other possible discretionary measures. Additional funds will also be required beyond this initial allocation, the magnitude of which will be determined by the eventual length of the restricted travel period.

Niue has developed a tourism recovery plan that aims to position the country as a safe and attractive travel destination upon the eventual resumption of international tourism. The plan is built upon sustained advertising and marketing, particularly in its main markets of New Zealand and Australia, with the aim of capturing a significant share of the first batches of tourists post-COVID-19. Prospects for economic recovery and easing of fiscal pressures will depend on how quickly international travel can resume, perhaps starting with Niue's potential inclusion in the trans-Tasman safe "travel bubble", or other similar arrangements. A critical prerequisite for this would be further strengthening of Niue's health system to allow for the implementation of strong protocols for testing, contact tracing, and medical care that will be shared across all parties to any efforts to restart international tourism.

Figure 10: Financing Needs for Niue's Economic Response to COVID-19

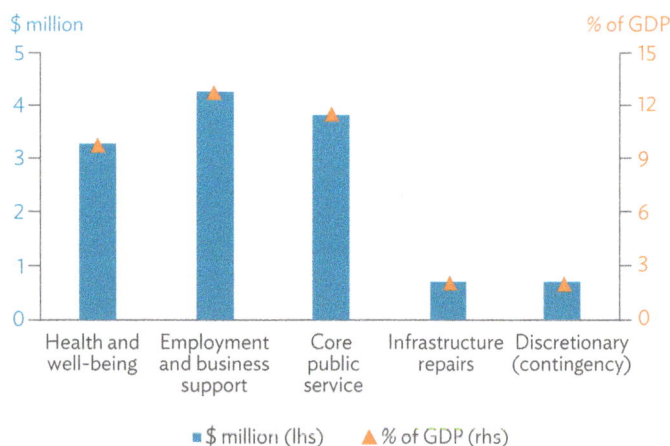

COVID-19 = coronavirus disease, GDP = gross domestic product, lhs = left-hand scale, rhs = right-hand scale.
Sources: Government of Niue. 2020. *Niue's Economic Response to COVID-19 Briefing Paper*. Alofi (April); and Asian Development Bank estimates.

References

Government of Niue. 2020. *Niue's Economic Response to COVID-19 Briefing Paper*. Alofi.

Palau: Bracing for an extended pause in tourism

Lead author: Rommel Rabanal

Global travel disruptions because of the COVID-19 pandemic are damaging Palau's vital tourism sector. Palau is among the most tourism-driven economies in the Pacific, with annual tourism receipts reaching the equivalent of 40%–50% of its gross domestic product. A tourist profile heavily tilted toward source markets in East Asia—in contrast to the dominance of tourism from Australia and New Zealand for South Pacific destinations—meant that Palau experienced adverse impacts of the COVID-19 pandemic before most of its subregional peers. The People's Republic of China (PRC) is the largest tourist market with a 32% share as of FY2019 (ended 30 September), followed by Japan (22%), Taipei,China (16%), and the Republic of Korea (13%). During the first 4 months of Palau's current fiscal year from October 2019 to January 2020, visitor arrivals were rising by almost 30% relative to its previous fiscal year. However, with the COVID-19 pandemic restricting tourism, first from the PRC and later from the other major markets, total arrivals fell by 43% year-on-year in February 2020 and plunged by 70% in March 2020.

These declines amplified the downturn in tourism that Palau had been experiencing already. From a peak of nearly 170,000 tourists (for a tourist-to-resident ratio of 9.5, among the highest globally) in FY2015, total arrivals steadily decreased to under 90,000 by FY2019. The decline was precipitated by a drought which affected water supply in hotels and resorts, while also decimating the jellyfish population in Palau's famed Jellyfish Lake that resulted in its temporary closure, thereby discouraging some tourists from visiting. Arrivals were further dented by tighter restrictions on tour groups from the PRC. Delta Airlines terminated regular flights from Tokyo in May 2018, followed by the indefinite suspension of Palau Pacific Airways' charter flights from Hong Kong, China in July of the same year. Given tourism's importance as the main driver of the Palau economy, the ongoing downturn has translated into economic contractions during FY2016, FY2017, and FY2019. Growth was only recorded in FY2018 because the economy was boosted by the advent of high-speed broadband internet services.

With minimal arrivals for an extended period in FY2020, inbound tourism is now expected to decline for a fifth consecutive year, possibly by as much as 49.9% to under 46,000. This could see Palau's economy contracting by as much as 9.5% in FY2020. Although tourism may recover in FY2021, the government's COVID-19 response plans are prudently based on the assumption that international travel will remain restricted until a vaccine becomes available in late 2021. This would likely result in a further contraction of 12.8%.

Although these plans will mitigate direct health impacts from the COVID-19 pandemic, they can also exact severe economic costs. The depth of projected annual economic contractions is nearly double those seen during the global financial and economic crisis of 2008–2009 that similarly saw drastically reduced tourist numbers traveling to Palau (Figure 11). Further, the cumulative FY2020–FY2021 economic contractions projected under an extended scenario would push per capita nominal incomes back below the FY2012 level.

Depressed economic activity will translate to massive job losses. The pre-pandemic tourism downturn already took its toll on the labor market, with employment falling by 1.7% in FY2019. This was the first decline since FY2011 and was mainly in tourism-linked sectors, including hotels and restaurants, transport, and retail trade. An extended border closure is projected to lead to the loss of over 3,100 jobs—or more than a quarter of formal employment—by the end of FY2021. Over two thirds of job losses are expected to arise from the closure of businesses with heavy linkages to a now-stagnant tourism sector.

In response to the potential impacts of the COVID-19 pandemic on businesses and workers, the government established a $20 million Coronavirus Relief One Stop Shop (CROSS) program to provide temporary assistance to the private sector. Direct relief measures under the program include (i) loans to businesses to cover fixed costs and possibly finance improvements in tourism facilities; (ii) unemployment benefits for workers whose employment has been terminated, suspended, or reduced; (iii) temporary employment schemes administered through the public sector and nongovernment organizations, particularly targeting nonresident workers; and (iv) expanded lifeline utility services to cover COVID-19-affected households.

Figure 11: Palau Visitor Arrivals
(FY2014–FY2019 actuals, by source economy; FY2020–FY2021 projections, various scenarios)

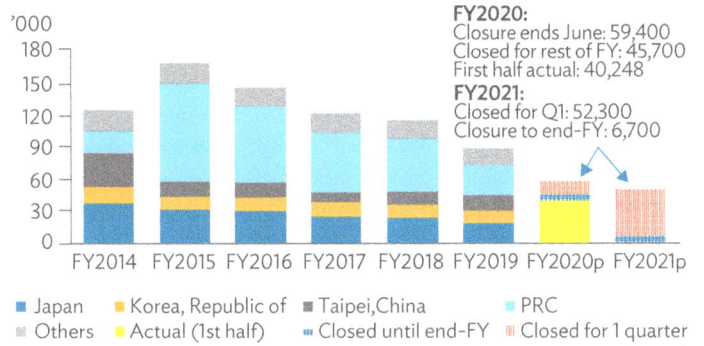

FY2020:
Closure ends June: 59,400
Closed for rest of FY: 45,700
First half actual: 40,248
FY2021:
Closed for Q1: 52,300
Closure to end-FY: 6,700

Legend: Japan; Korea, Republic of; Taipei,China; PRC; Others; Actual (1st half); Closed until end-FY; Closed for 1 quarter

FY = fiscal year, p = projection, PRC = People's Republic of China, Q = quarter.
Note: Projections reflect scenarios where global restrictions on international travel are in effect until June 2020 (closed for 1 quarter FY2020, consistent with *Asian Development Outlook 2020*); September 2020 (closed until end FY2020); December 2020 (closed for 1 quarter FY2021); and September 2021 (closed until end FY2021).
Sources: Palau Bureau of Budget and Planning and Asian Development Bank estimates.

Figure 12: Palau Economic Performance and Prospects
(FY2005–FY2021, under extended travel restrictions scenario)

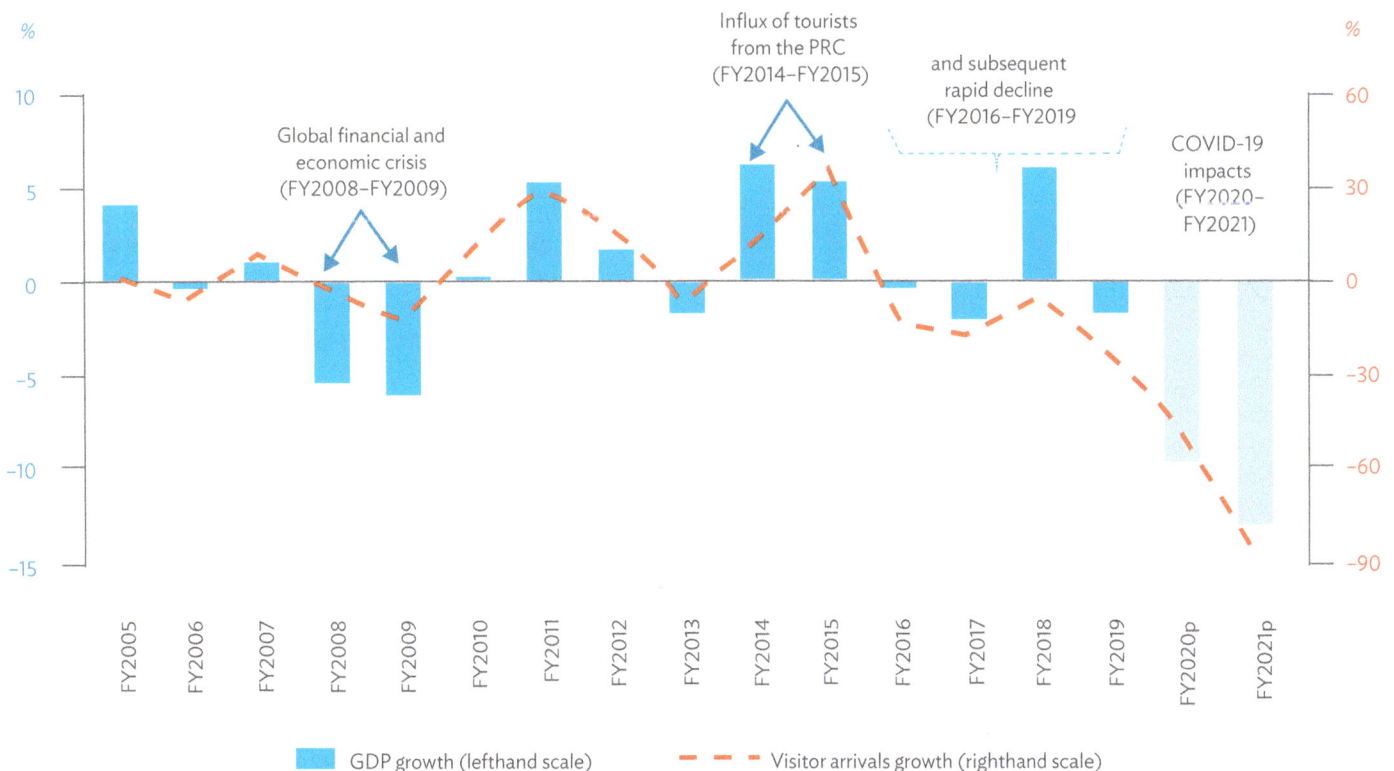

GDP growth (lefthand scale)   Visitor arrivals growth (righthand scale)

COVID-19 = coronavirus disease, FY = fiscal year, GDP = gross domestic product, PRC = People's Republic of China, p = projection.
Sources: Asian Development Outlook database and Graduate School USA. *2020. Assessing the Impact of COVID-19 on the Palauan Economy. Economic Monitoring and Analysis Program (EconMAP) Technical Note.* https://pitiviti.org/news/wp-content/uploads/downloads/2020/04/EconFiscImpact_COVID-19_Mar2020_Web.pdf (March).

The CROSS program's work to support tourism businesses and retain migrant workers in-country bolsters Palau's capacity to bounce back quickly after the COVID-19 crisis. From a broader perspective, Palau's efforts to further develop as a high-value and sustainable tourism destination will contribute also to facilitating swift economic recovery. These include (i) ongoing and planned investments in the water supply and sanitation, as well as renewable energy sectors to safeguard Palau's pristine environment; (ii) preparation of a comprehensive urban development strategy for Babeldaob, Palau's largest yet sparsely populated island, as the next frontier of sustainable tourism development; and (iii) development of information and communication technology applications that harness improved internet connectivity to enhance visitors' experience. Palau should consider fully integrating comprehensive "build back better" approaches to tourism-led recovery, including alignment with the Secretariat of the Pacific Regional Environment Programme's call to feature environmental sustainability considerations in members' COVID-19 recovery plans.

References

Government of Palau. 2020. *The Coronavirus Relief One-Stop Shop Act or CROSS Act.* Republic of Palau Public Law 10-56. Koror.

Graduate School USA. 2020. *Assessing the impact of COVID-19 on the Palauan economy.* https://pitiviti.org/news/wp-content/uploads/downloads/2020/04/EconFiscImpact_COVID-19_Mar2020_Web.pdf

Impact of COVID-19 on Economy and Poverty in Papua New Guinea and the Government's Response Plan

Lead author: Magdelyn Kuari

At the end of March 2020, Papua New Guinea (PNG) had its first confirmed case of COVID-19. The government issued a state of national emergency to respond to the COVID-19 outbreak (Box). Because of a weak health system and the vulnerability of the country's economy to external shocks, COVID-19 increases health and poverty risks and challenges the economic stability of the country. This article examines the impact of COVID-19 on the economy by focusing on the macroeconomic indicators, small and medium-sized enterprises, and poverty in PNG; and the government's efforts in responding to the pandemic through the stimulus package plan.

IMPACT ON THE ECONOMY

Economic growth. ADB forecasts that the PNG economy will contract by 1.5% in 2020 (ADB 2020a). Transport and storage, accommodation and food services, real estate, and construction have all been impacted by the temporary shutdown of the economy. Agriculture is expected to perform poorly because of weaker external demand, lower commodity prices, and disruptions to transportation

---

Box: Papua New Guinea Measures Taken During the State of National Emergency

The Government of Papua New Guinea declared a state of emergency on 23 March 2020 following the first confirmed COVID-19 case in the country. The state of emergency included lockdown with restrictions to movements, including a ban on international and domestic travels, partial business operation, and temporary shutdown of schools and social activities, such as sports, and religious and cultural gatherings. The state of emergency lasted until 16 June 2020 and there have been 30 confirmed cases as of 23 July 2020. A period of hard lockdown lasted from the end of March through April, with gradual reopening of the economy thereafter, although, as of June, borders remain closed and international flights largely suspended.

Source: Government of Papua New Guinea Official COVID-19 Website. https://covid19.info.gov.pg/.

---

and trade partly because of quarantine requirements on shipments that have affected turnaround times. Oil and gas exporters have been hit hard by lower international prices, with at least one major oil exporter announcing staff layoffs. The 2020 production targets for liquefied natural gas, PNG's largest export, have not been significantly revised, indicating largely undisrupted operations. Likewise, gold mines are expected to maintain the usual levels of production, additionally buoyed by a rising gold price. Key fly-in, fly-out workers for extractives industries were quickly placed on travel exemption lists. However, suspension of mining operations at the Porgera Gold Mine—which was not caused by COVID-19—will significantly affect gold production overall in 2020.

Balance of payments. Consequently, PNG's balance of trade position will deteriorate in 2020. Export earnings are expected to fall from the equivalent of 45.6% of GDP in 2019 to 38.0% of GDP in 2020, significantly reducing the current account surplus from 22.3% of GDP in 2019 to 14.6% of GDP in 2020. As a result, there is increased downward pressure on foreign exchange reserves (which stood at $2.3 billion in December 2019, or 6.0 months of import cover) and availability of foreign exchange in the commercial market, with some businesses now months behind on paying suppliers.

Inflation. Inflationary pressures from the COVID-19 pandemic are mixed. There will be downside pressures because of lower oil prices as well as weaker domestic demand associated with a loss of income and reduced spending. Additionally, the government introduced price control measures for basic consumer items during the state of national emergency period, and a freight subsidy program was introduced for shipment of local produce to the capital that resulted in a large supply response of fruits and vegetables. However, there is also upward pressure on prices because of increased scarcity of goods and higher depreciative pressure on the exchange rate. Additionally, the central bank introduced a program of quantitative easing, which may increase money supply. Inflation for 2020 is projected at 3.3%.

Fiscal position. The government now anticipates a revenue shortfall of about K2.2 billion (2.7% of GDP) for 2020 compared with initial budget estimates. Additional expenditure is needed to implement the government's COVID-19 emergency and response plan, although the government has indicated that funding for this will be reallocated from other sources. The fiscal deficit for 2020 is now projected to be about 7.6% of GDP, up from 4.9% in 2019 and a budget estimate of 5.0% of GDP. This would result in debt increasing to more than 45% of GDP, the ceiling for 2020 set under the Fiscal Responsibility Act (amended 2019).

IMPACT ON SMALL AND MEDIUM-SIZED ENTERPRISES

Under the lockdown, movement of people between provinces was restricted and a ban imposed on international flights. These restrictions severely affected the incomes of businesses engaged in travel, tourism, restaurants, hotels, and construction, and resulted in job losses.

Similarly, income of small and medium-sized enterprises (SMEs) directly linked to these sectors, e.g., tour operators, florists, cleaning, agriculture, fishing, and arts and culture, has been affected. Transportation and logistics issues, inability to meet rental or loan payments, and lack of customers because of social distancing are some of the issues also affecting the SMEs.

A survey conducted by the PNG Business Council of 300 businesses in 20 sectors and 10 provinces during March–May 2020 revealed that respondents estimate that they experienced about 50% lower revenue and net profit during the survey period as a direct result of the COVID-19 restrictions from late March to April.

IMPACT ON POVERTY

The COVID-19 pandemic increases risks for the poor and vulnerable. PNG's social indicators are below those of other countries with similar per capita incomes. PNG is ranked 155th out of 189 countries in the 2019 Human Development Index. There have been reports that the lockdown affected food security, health, education, and family protection.

Jobs, income, and food security. The most vulnerable are low-income earners (especially those earning at or below the minimum wage), those in small businesses, those who engage in informal activity such as market and street vendors, and those whose livelihood depends on border crossing areas. As of 2017, 37.5% of PNG's population lives below the national poverty line (ADB 2020b). The COVID-19 pandemic increases the risk of pushing more people into poverty.

Food access by the urban population has been affected by the loss of jobs and income resulting from the impact of the pandemic on the economy. This increases the risk of hunger and associated health and nutrition issues for this group. In general, the population also faces the risk of supply shortage from both import sources and domestic production because of quarantine requirements for shipments, restrictions imposed by major producing countries for basic food supply such as rice and wheat for their own consumption, and supply of domestic produce (mainly vegetables and fruits

from the Highlands region) being affected by the travel ban. Food donation and community support to impacted villages and cities have been of great assistance during the lockdown. However, without a sustainable food security program, the population will continue to face food security issues during times of natural and artificial shocks like disasters and pandemics (e.g. COVID-19).

Health, education, and family protection. Although there have been only 30 confirmed cases and no deaths (as of 23 July 2020), an assessment developed by the National Department of Health and the World Health Organization for PNG's COVID-19 Multi Sector Response Plan for a worst-case scenario suggests that one in five Papua New Guineans could become infected in this COVID-19 pandemic. The most vulnerable populations are older people, infants and children, and people with complicating conditions such as diabetes, heart or respiratory diseases, or compromised immune systems, populations with tuberculosis (TB) or HIV, concentrated or highly mobile populations, and communities with inadequate access to proper hygiene supplies or inadequate hygiene practices. There are about 50,000 people living with HIV/AIDS in PNG, of which only about half are regularly taking medication, and about 37,000 people living with TB. PNG has high burdens of TB, multidrug-resistant TB, and TB/HIV coinfection, exposing this segment of the population to high risks (PNG DMT 2020).

Education, specifically student learning, has been affected by the COVID-19 pandemic because of limited opportunities to use alternate teaching methods such as virtual learning or e-learning. Since the lockdown, operations in almost all educational institutions have been temporarily suspended. According to the National Research Institute, close to 50 days of teaching time are estimated to have been lost because of the lockdown. This is expected to make 30,000 students in grades 8, 10, and 12 ineligible for progression to the next level of education (Auka-Salmang 2020a). Overcrowded classrooms, with a teacher-to-pupil ratio of 1:50/60, increases the risk of spreading COVID-19 especially among the younger population (Devette-Chee 2020).

The state of national emergency has also taken a toll on women and girls, who have experienced violence in their homes. According to UN Women Papua New Guinea, PNG ranks very low in all global indicators in advancing gender equality and elimination of violence against women. There is increasing gender-based violence and disruptions to accessing health, safety, security, transport, and justice services as government institutions shifted resources to addressing the pandemic (Auka-Salmang 2020b).

RESPONSES TO THE COVID-19 PANDEMIC

Government response. To address the health, economic, and poverty challenges as a result of the COVID-19 pandemic, the government announced a funding package in early April 2020 comprising the following:

- K2.5 billion in additional treasury bonds and bills, to help with deficit financing and pay amortizations that are due in 2020;
- K0.6 billion credit support to commercial banks, to facilitate debt relief for businesses and households;

- K1.5 billion in additional support being sought from ADB, the IMF, the World Bank, and the Government of Australia, which will be spent toward deficit financing;
- K0.5 billion in superannuation payments to support the unemployed, which will be aided by the Bank of Papua New Guinea's quantitative easing; and
- K0.6 billion in direct budget support to COVID-19 response, which includes K250 million for health and K250 million for other economic projects.

The government raised a K2 billion domestic treasury bond in May at yields from 8.0% to 9.5% for tenors of 2, 3, and 5 years and 12.5% for tenors of 10 years. The balance is expected to be raised in June. The success of the K2 billion treasury bond COVID-19 financing allowed the government to approve K600 million, comprising K280 million to support health and security and K320 million to support agriculture, households, and business. Some of the major areas in health and security to receive funding support are K60 million for upgrading hygiene at potential COVID-19 hotspots; K67 million to support frontline health workers and purchase personal protective equipment and other vital health support; K133 million to strengthen law and order and security; K15 million to build capacity at overseas posts and help repatriate PNG citizens; and K5 million in administrative support for churches and city/urban authorities to provide food for those most in need. The K320.0 million support to agriculture, households, and business includes K113.0 million to promote agriculture development and food security; K50.0 million for a price support program for small cash crop producers of coffee, cocoa, and copra; K45.5 million to support rural microenterprises, SMEs, and households; K41.5 million to support logistics and freight, and pay outstanding government debt to small business; and K70.0 million for additional economic stimulus activities to be determined by the government in consultation with other agencies and businesses.

ADB response. ADB's response to COVID-19 includes an expected grant under the Asia Pacific Disaster Response Fund, which can be used to support immediate lifesaving response measures. In addition, ADB plans to provide additional direct budget support through the Health Services Sector Development Program policy-based loan and is considering additional financing through the COVID-19 Pandemic Response Option modality. Key ADB-funded international health consultants are supporting the National Department of Health in the COVID-19 response. Other ongoing assistance has been mostly to provide financing as well as technical assistance through the technical assistance for Supporting Public Financial Management.

Concluding Remarks

PNG is likely to continue facing economic challenges and poverty risks as a result of COVID-19. The pandemic's impact on the health, economy, and poverty in the country will depend on how the government responds to protect the health of the people while, at the same time, navigating the economy away from falling into recession and pushing the vulnerable into poverty. Timely securing and releasing of funds, effective implementation of the government's response plan, and partnership with development partners, civil society, and the local community are all key to achieving desired outcomes.

References

ADB. 2020a. *Asian Development Outlook 2020 Supplement: Lockdown, Loosening, and Asia's Growth Prospects.* Manila.

ADB. 2020b. *Basic Statistics 2020.* Manila.

Auka-Salmang, G. 2020a. *NRI: Current Mode of Teaching to Affect Students in the Long Run.* Post Courier. https://postcourier.com.pg/nri-current-mode-of-teaching-to-affect-students-inlong-run/.

Auka-Salmang, G. 2020b. *Rise in Violence During SoE: Report.* Post Courier. https://postcourier.com.pg/rise-in-violence-during-soe-report/.

Devette-Chee, K. 2020. *Preventive Measures Against the Spread of COVID-19 in Papua New Guinea Schools: Is it Time to Reopen Schools?* The Papua New Guinea National Research Institute. Spotlight Volume 13, Issue 5. https://pngnri.org/images/Publications/Spotlight_Vol_13_Issue_5_Preventive_measures_against_the_spread_of_COVID-19_in_Papua_New_Guinea_schools.pdf.

Papua New Guinea Disaster Management Team (PNG DMT). 2020. *COVID-19 Multi Sector Response Plan.* Port Moresby. https://reliefweb.int/sites/reliefweb.int/files/resources/200521%20DMT%20COVID-19%20HRP.pdf.

Samoa and Tonga: Recoveries Interrupted, Risks Realized

Lead author: James Webb

As with almost all nations around the world, COVID-19 is the largest economic challenge in the living memory of Samoa and Tonga. With the borders closed, the public rightly risk-averse, and fiscal resources stretched, there is little that governments can do to directly address the local impacts from the global contraction. However, the COVID-19 economic crisis has been made even more severe through the additional impacts of recent natural and public health disasters. In any other year, the measles outbreak would have been the defining crisis for Samoa, and Tropical Cyclone Harold for Tonga. COVID-19 has highlighted that Tonga and Samoa, like most Pacific island countries, face multiple risks to development, with repeated and overlapping economic shocks demonstrating how fragile development gains can be. The realization of these risks has deepened the already severe impacts of the global pandemic on the local economies, particularly tourism. With COVID-19 likely to affect economic growth for some time to come, mitigating other sources of risk is a crucial way that authorities can limit the overall impact on livelihoods and economic growth from this and future crises.

TWIN PUBLIC HEALTH CRISES FOR SAMOA

On 22 October 2019, Samoa declared a measles outbreak, confirming fears that low vaccination rates could lead to widespread community transmission. By the time the outbreak was under control in January 2020 through a large vaccination effort, there had been over 5,700 cases and 83 deaths, most of whom were children. The outbreak sent shockwaves throughout the region and would prove to be a touchstone for the COVID-19 crisis that was still in its infancy. When COVID-19 did eventually arrive in the Pacific, almost all countries moved rapidly to close their borders, shaken by what had transpired only months earlier. For Samoa, however, it meant that what should have been a period of recovery for the tourism industry became a prolonged and much deeper crisis.

Samoa visitor arrivals had been a strong source of economic growth in previous years, increasing by 11.6% in FY2018 (ended 30 June for both Samoa and Tonga) and a further 9.3% in FY2019. This impressive growth rapidly reversed during the measles outbreak, with growth in arrivals slowing to 0.1% in October 2019 from the previous year (Figure 13). The contraction in visitor arrivals that followed in December 2019 through to February 2020 was, at the time, the largest contraction on record.

Figure 13: Successive health crises have reversed rapid tourism growth in Samoa. (y-o-y % growth in visitor arrivals)

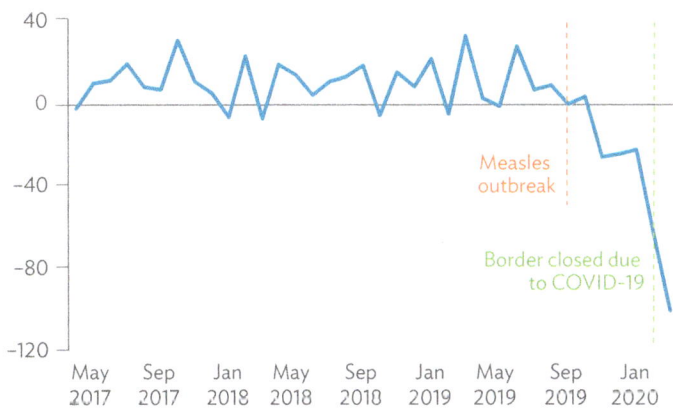

COVID-19 = coronavirus disease, y-o-y = year on year.
Source: Central Bank of Samoa.

This pre-COVID contraction in visitor arrivals had a marked effect on private business conditions. For example, the Development Bank of Samoa had about 25% of nonperforming loans in 2017, 60% of which were in the tourism sector (ADB 2019).This exposure was partly a result of the government using the Development Bank of Samoa to finance disaster recovery efforts from Tropical Cyclone Gita, many of which were directed at the tourism sector. In mid-2019, the government mandated a delay on the foreclosure of several large nonperforming loans to avoid possible economic disruption, against the backdrop of increasing tourist demand. While this meant that some of these loans may have been able to be recovered, the measles outbreak more than reversed any progress, and other tourism operators (who were, prior to the measles outbreak, current on repayments) also began to approach their financial institutions for credit relief. With widespread restrictions related to COVID-19 from March 2020, all tourism businesses will face increasingly severe conditions and heightened financial stress, reversing years of development, further damaging the viability of many businesses in the industry, and putting the Samoan finance

sector under severe stress. With borders unlikely to open before December 2020, the dual public health crises effectively extended the period of difficulty for the economy by at least 4 months, with sectors exposed to tourism experiencing almost 15 months of historic declines. In addition, remittances have slowed from 21.0% growth in FY2018 and 10.1% in FY2019 to just 0.5% growth in the 12 months to April 2020, providing little to balance the abrupt contraction in tourism income. Overall, GDP is expected to contract by 5.0% in FY2020, with an additional 2.0% contraction in FY2021, despite the anticipated gradual recommencement of travel early in the new year.

COVID-19 COMPOUNDS CLIMATE RISKS IN TONGA

For Tonga, Tropical Cyclone Gita devastated the country in 2018, causing an estimated $164 million in damage (equivalent to 38% of GDP). The International Monetary Fund estimated that reconstruction would contribute to GDP growth of about 3.0% in FY2019, but this was later revised to 0.7% because of project delays. The expectation was that this activity would occur in FY2020, but this was disrupted by COVID-19 which extended mobilization periods and reduced the economic benefits in buffering the global downturn. Construction was also delayed by Tropical Cyclone Sarai in December 2019, Tropical Cyclone Tino in January 2020, and a further $24.8 million in damages and further delays caused by Tropical Cyclone Harold in April 2020. Taken together, these disruptions present a significant challenge to infrastructure and reconstruction timelines (and their associated economic and community benefits) despite the best efforts of development partners and the government to coordinate project continuity.

As elsewhere, COVID-19 has also seriously disrupted a nascent recovery in visitor arrivals. After falling by 10.7% in 2018 because of Tropical Cyclone Gita, visitor arrivals had shown a strong recovery in 2019, growing by 14.3% in the year-to-September. While a recovery in international travel after COVID-19 appears uncertain at this stage, having the necessary infrastructure and assets in place to capture any tourism growth are crucial for economic recovery. Unfortunately, the storm surge from Tropical Cyclone Harold destroyed three hotels in the coastal areas of Tongatapu, adding to the already difficult task that Tonga will face in reaping any dividends from the oft-discussed Pacific "travel bubble" or eventual recovery in international travel. The economy is expected to contract by 3.0% in FY2020 because of the decline in tourism, with a further 4.0% decline in FY2021 because of continued challenges in tourism and weak local demand.

THE TYRANNY OF OVERLAPPING DISASTERS

The fiscal, economic, and public health challenges in both nations are extreme, and will require a timely and prudent application of government fiscal measures. However, the incumbent risks to development still present significant risks in their own right. Climate change and natural hazards have rightly attracted much of policymakers' attention, as most recently highlighted in Tonga, particularly in the areas of early warning, immediate recovery, and financial planning, which should be celebrated as key enablers of reducing the loss of life and speeding the immediate recovery following a disaster. Samoa, too, showed impressive mobilization to vaccinate 94% of the population against measles by January 2020. However, COVID-19 will put unprecedented pressure on fiscal resources, limiting the types of possible interventions that can be made in response to other emerging needs. Development partners have a key role to play in supplementing government efforts, but will also face challenges in responding to multiple, simultaneous crises. ADB is itself a demonstration of this: of the $18.6 million disbursed for disaster response in Tonga since the start of 2020, $0.2 million is related to the category 4 Tropical Cyclone Harold, with the remainder dedicated to addressing COVID-19.

REDUCING INCUMBENT RISKS

For the respective governments, with public finance under increasing strain, an alternative approach may be to focus on mitigating key risks without creating the need for significant additional outlays. In doing so, governments may limit future instances where overlapping, concurrent risks lead to multiple social and economic disasters. An example of this is in relation to noncommunicable diseases (NCDs), which are shown to increase the risk of severe illness if present in persons infected with COVID-19 (WHO 2020a). Conversely, good health is a benefit to economic growth through increased worker productivity, reduced absenteeism, increased educational outcomes, and reduced or postponed use of medical resources—freeing up financial space for other purposes. At the household level, good health—and good health systems—helps individuals maximize their human potential, avoid financial distress and impoverishment, and break the inter-generational cycle of maternal ill health, impaired productivity of children, and consequential poverty. The global evidence increasingly shows that NCDs result in long-term macroeconomic impacts on labor supply, capital accumulation, and GDP growth (World Bank 2016).

In Tonga, 74.0% of the population aged 18–69 has been diagnosed with an NCD, and an estimated 98.7% of this demographic is at moderate to high risk of developing one (WHO 2014). It was estimated that 90.7% of the population were overweight, 67.6% were obese, 27.6% had hypertension, 34.4% had elevated levels of blood glucose, and 48.8% had elevated levels of blood cholesterol. For Samoa, almost 100% of the population is estimated to be at moderate to high risk of developing an NCD: 84.7% of the population is estimated to be overweight, 63.1% obese, 24.8% to have diabetes, and 24.5% hypertension (WHO and Government of Samoa 2013). About 70% of total deaths in Samoa are attributable to NCDs. Its treatment puts disproportionate pressure on government health financing via expensive treatment options, and the burden of NCDs on GDP is estimated at 5.6%–8.5% in Samoa and 8.3%–12.3% in Tonga. About 12.4% of the effective labor force in Samoa and 18.5% in Tonga is expected to be lost by 2040 through a combination of morbidity and early death (World Bank 2016).

Cost-effective interventions, like the World Health Organization's Package of Essential NCD (PEN), target early detection, management, and community awareness of NCDs through community-based participation and integrated village outreach services. The locally adapted "PEN Fa'a Samoa" model has shown positive results, with over 92% of the target population reached and screened for NCDs, among which almost 45% were found to have risk factors for NCDs, and almost 20% have reported possible symptoms of cardiovascular disease and diabetes. This results in better treatment options and early intervention, reducing both the lifetime impacts on households and cost to the government. Other measures may include targeted reductions in the consumption of alcohol, tobacco, high-fat, high-salt, and high-sugar foods through control measures, such as taxation, increased uptake of local food alternatives, and improved community outreach programs to induce change in dietary patterns and promote physical activity. Taxation measures, particularly on tobacco and alcohol, have been shown to be highly effective at both reducing usage and increasing government revenue (WHO 2011). This is especially important with tobacco use, which is shown to increase the severity of COVID-19 symptoms (WHO 2020b).

More broadly, with elevated uncertainty around how long the COVID-19 crisis will last, any reduction in risk profile will increase the ability of Samoa and Tonga to weather this and future crises. In particular, with its associated COVID-19 coinfection risk, NCD prevalence may be a sensible and low-cost area that the governments may wish to increase their policy focus on. Tax measures on harmful products may be particularly appealing in this fiscally constrained environment.

References

ADB. 2019. *Finding Balance 2019: Benchmarking the Performance of State-Owned Banks in the Pacific.* Manila.

World Bank. 2016. *Health & non-communicable diseases.* Pacific Possible Series. Washington D.C.

World Health Organization (WHO). 2011. *Technical Manual on Tobacco Tax Administration.* Geneva.

WHO. 2014. *Kingdom of Tonga NCD Risk Factors STEPS Report 2014.* Suva.

WHO. 2020a. *COVID-19: vulnerable and high-risk groups.* https://www.who.int/westernpacific/emergencies/covid-19/information/high-risk-groups.

WHO. 2020b. *Smoking and COVID-19 – Scientific Brief.* Geneva.

WHO and Government of Samoa. 2013. *STEPwise Surveillance of Risk Factors.* Apia.

Twin shocks: Dealing with COVID-19 and Tropical Cyclone Harold in Solomon Islands and Vanuatu

Lead authors: Jacqueline Connell and Prince Cruz

Aside from the socioeconomic impacts of COVID-19, Solomon Islands and Vanuatu are also grappling with the effects of Tropical Cyclone Harold, which crossed the Pacific in early April. Passing through Solomon Islands as a category 3 cyclone before strengthening to category 5 as it reached Vanuatu, it resulted in loss of lives, left thousands homeless, and damaged livelihoods and infrastructure in both countries. Disaster response and relief efforts were hampered by travel and transport restrictions which were imposed because of COVID-19.

The economic impact of the simultaneous shocks has been immense and both economies are forecast to contract in 2020, following a decade of uninterrupted growth (ADB 2020a). Tourism and trade have been reduced by COVID-19 containment measures and the global economic slowdown, while agriculture has been ravaged by the cyclone. The employment, poverty, and social impacts could also be large. Using International Labour Organization estimates, 75% of women were found to be in vulnerable employment in both countries, where they are unlikely to have formal working arrangements (World Bank 2020). Even for those in the formal sector, there is no unemployment insurance to support people who lose their jobs.

Despite the economic impact of COVID-19 containment measures, decisive and proactive measures to prevent COVID-19 from entering Solomon Islands and Vanuatu were warranted, given the countries' limited health systems. There were less than two physicians for every 10,000 people in both countries, among the lowest in the Pacific (Table 2, page 28). Also, the number of hospital beds, and nurses and midwives per 10,000 people were lower than the average number for Pacific small island states (Table 3).

Table 3: Comparative Data on Health Care Facilities and Personnel
(per 10,000 population)

Item	Solomon Islands	Vanuatu	Pacific Small Island States
Hospital beds	14.0	17.0	20.8
Nurses and midwives	21.6	14.2	28.0
Physicians	1.9	1.7	5.0

Notes: Data as of 2018 for nurses and midwives, 2016 for physicians, and for hospitals beds: 2012 for Solomon Islands and 2008 for Vanuatu. Pacific small island states include Fiji, Kiribati, the Marshall Islands, the Federated States of Micronesia, Nauru, Palau, Samoa, Solomon Islands, Tonga, Tuvalu, and Vanuatu. Source: World Bank. *World Development Indicators.* https://data.worldbank.org/.

If COVID-19 was to arrive and spread, the health impacts could be severe with only 25% of the population in Vanuatu and 36% in Solomon Islands using basic handwashing facilities with soap and water

as of 2017 (World Bank 2020). A wide gap between rural and urban areas was observed in both countries, with less people in rural areas with handwashing facilities. Further, less than 35% of the population in Solomon Islands and Vanuatu was using basic sanitation services. These conditions were far worse than the average for Pacific small island states with 69% of the population on average using basic sanitation.

SOLOMON ISLANDS

To prevent the spread of COVID-19, the Government of Solomon Islands restricted entry from countries with COVID-19 infections on 1 February. The government then declared a state of emergency on 25 March, suspended all international passenger flights, and imposed strict quarantine measures on incoming cargo ships. Citizens in Honiara, the capital, were encouraged to return to their home islands. Public services were scaled down and schools were temporarily closed.

The impacts of COVID-19 were exacerbated by Tropical Cyclone Harold, which crossed the islands from 1 to 4 April, affecting Honiara and several provinces. A ship carrying evacuees from Honiara to Malaita Province was hit by a storm surge that led to the death of 27 people on 2 April. More than 30% of the population were estimated to have been affected by a combination of strong wind, heavy rainfall, and flooding (ADB 2020b).

The economy of Solomon Islands is projected to contract by 6.0% in 2020—the first contraction since 2009. Agriculture is expected to see a significant decline in crop production, forestry, and fishery. Contributions to growth from industry and services are also expected to be negative (Figure 14).

Figure 14: Solomon Islands Supply-Side Contributions to GDP Growth

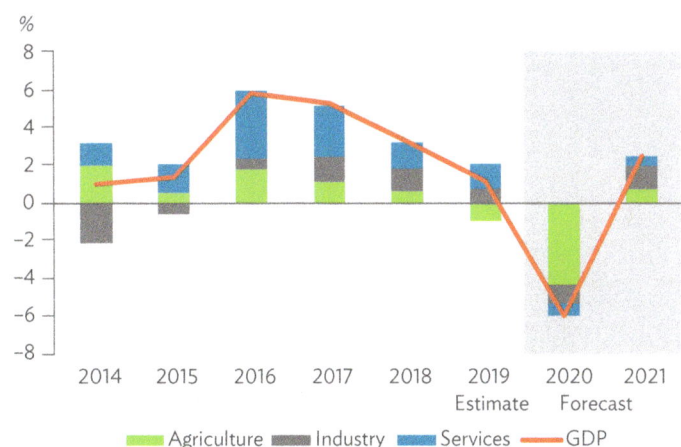

GDP = gross domestic product.
Sources: Solomon Islands National Statistics Office; and Asian Development Bank estimates.

Solomon Islands' merchandise exports were equal to about one-third of its GDP in 2018, more than any other Pacific developing member country, excluding Papua New Guinea. The global economic slowdown caused by COVID-19 is expected to decrease demand for the country's exports, particularly from the People's Republic of China, the destination for 65% of merchandise exports in 2019.

Damage from Tropical Cyclone Harold is expected to reduce agricultural output, which supplies most of the country's merchandise exports (Figure 15). Log and timber output, which supplied 72% of exports in 2019, was down to 78,000 cubic meters in April 2020, significantly lower than the average monthly output of 225,000 cubic meters in 2018 and 2019. The fish catch, which supplied 11% of exports in 2019, was down to 1.1 million metric tons in April, from a monthly average of 3.4 million metric tons in 2018 and 2019.

In addition to a decline in merchandise exports, tourism receipts and remittances are projected to fall. Although lower oil imports, largely because of lower oil prices, should provide some offset, the current account deficit is expected to increase substantially. In part, this will be funded by greater development partner support, but foreign reserves are predicted to fall. However, reserves remain high and, in May 2020, the Central Bank of Solomon Islands reported that gross international reserves provided 12.7 months of import cover, well above its minimum threshold of 6.0 months.

Weaker economic activity, combined with lower global commodity prices, may ease inflation pressures in 2020. However, inflation increased to 7.7% during the first 4 months, likely reflecting supply chain disruptions and increased demand for domestic items (Figure 16). The index for alcoholic beverages and tobacco, which account for 12.4% of the consumer basket, rose 47.9% over the same period. The index for health rose 9.1% because of the increase in medical consultation fees, while the index for food rose only 2.9%. In response, the government established price controls on basic commodities as part of the COVID-19 state of emergency in March. The Central Bank of Solomon Islands has loosened monetary policy stance to support the economy.

The government's fiscal response to COVID-19 consists of two components: a COVID-19 Preparedness and Response Plan, which provides for increased expenditure of up to the equivalent of 1.1% of GDP largely on health preparedness and containment measures; and an Economic Stimulus Package, which is equal to about 2.6% of GDP, focused on protecting jobs and stabilizing the economy. The Economic Stimulus Package, announced on 4 May, comprises short-term and medium-term measures, including social assistance to support the resumption of schools; tax extensions and rental relief for affected small and medium-sized enterprises; support for existing investments in agriculture, fishery, and forestry; public infrastructure investments in rural wharves and airports; and equity injections for the state-owned Solomon Airlines, Soltuna, and Solomon Water, as well as the Development Bank of Solomon Islands, which is expected to translate into concessional loans for affected businesses.

Figure 15: Solomon Islands Merchandise Exports

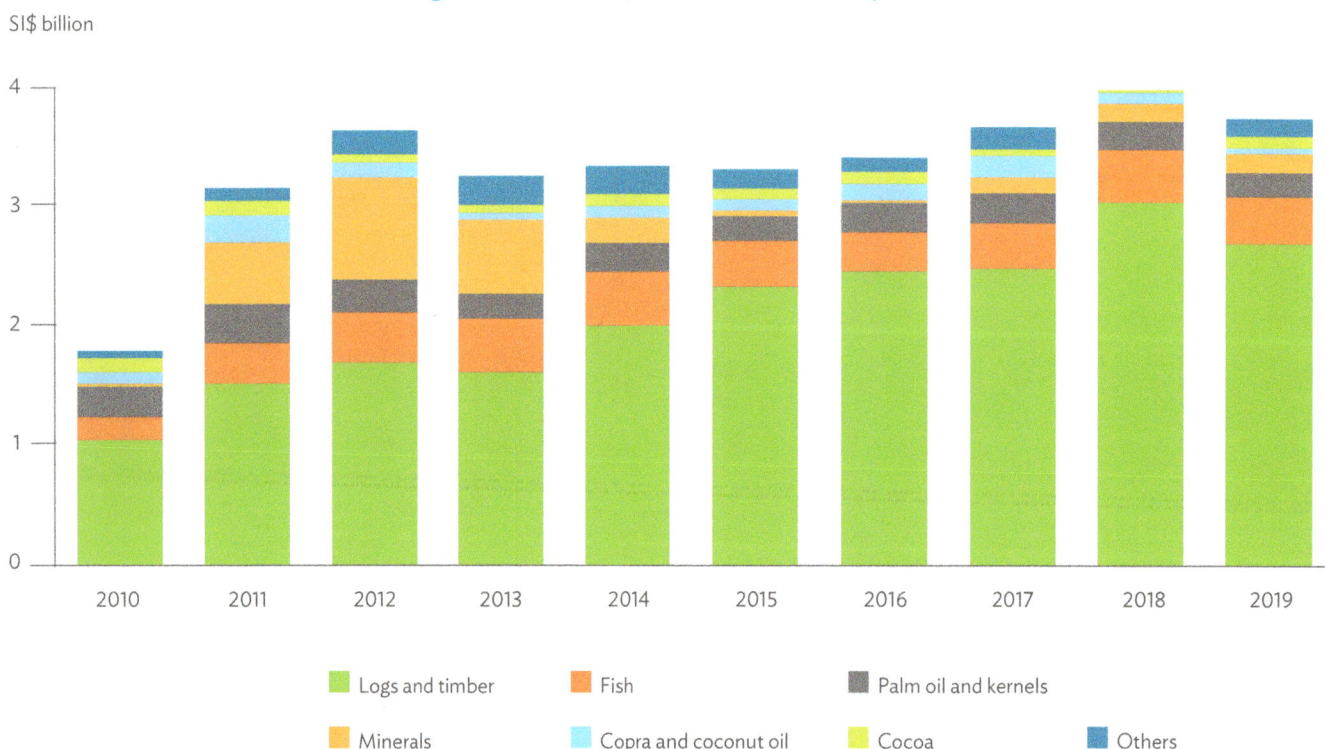

Source: Solomon Islands National Statistics Office.

Figure 16: Solomon Islands Inflation

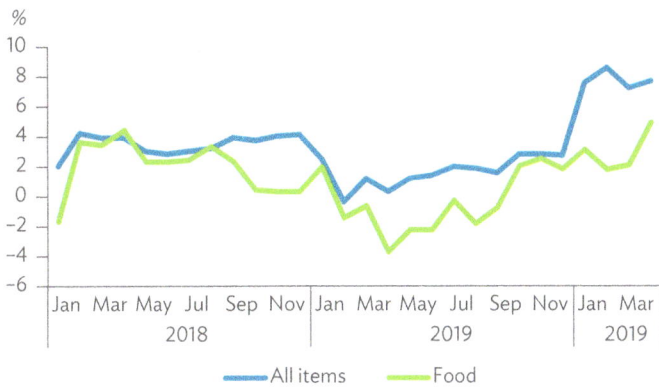

Source: Solomon Islands National Statistics Office.

Higher government spending, combined with lower revenues particularly from log export duties which supply some 20% of domestic revenues, is expected to push the fiscal deficit to the equivalent of about 6% of GDP in 2020, from 1.7% of GDP deficit in 2019. The government's fiscal buffers had fallen prior to 2020 and the IMF estimated that the government's cash balances narrowed to the equivalent of less than 1 month of recurrent spending in 2019. Development partner support in response to COVID-19 is likely to play a critical role in ensuring short-term budget stability, given the increasing fiscal pressures and large downside risks facing the economy in 2020. The fiscal response packages are expected to be financed partly by the issuance of domestic bonds, and by grants and loans from development partners. While public debt has been low, it is expected to rise considerably over the medium term. The IMF (2020) projects that the ratio of public debt to GDP will rise to 15.7% in 2020 from an estimated 8.9% the previous year, although the risk of debt distress remains moderate.

VANUATU

To prevent COVID-19 from entering Vanuatu, the government suspended all international flights on 20 March, and declared a state of emergency on 26 March 2020. On 5 April, Tropical Cyclone Harold made landfall on Espiritu Santo, the location of the second biggest city, Luganville. The cyclone damaged homes, schools, medical facilities, and other infrastructure. It also damaged agriculture, compromising food security and farmers' incomes, particularly in the provinces of Sanma, Penama, and Malampa. About 176,000 people—more than half the population—were affected and three people killed (FAO 2020).

ADB projects that the economy will contract by 9.8% in 2020 because of the combined impacts of COVID-19 and Tropical Cyclone Harold. This would be the worst contraction since it gained its independence in 1980. It also breaks more than a decade of uninterrupted economic growth. The main impact would be through the tourism sector, with travel and transport estimated to contribute 35.5% of GDP in 2018. Agriculture and industry are also expected to contract, while government-related services are seen to expand (Figure 17).

Prior to the shocks, tourism had a positive start for 2020 with arrivals by cruise ship jumping 65.4% year-on-year in the first quarter, although arrivals by air dropped 2.0% over the same period (Figure 18). For the rest of the year, visitor arrivals are assumed to be minimal given travel restrictions in Vanuatu's largest source markets: Australia and New Zealand. The prospect of a Pacific "travel bubble" holds some promise, although additional measures may be needed to help mitigate the risks to the local population.

Figure 17: Vanuatu Supply-Side Contributions to GDP growth

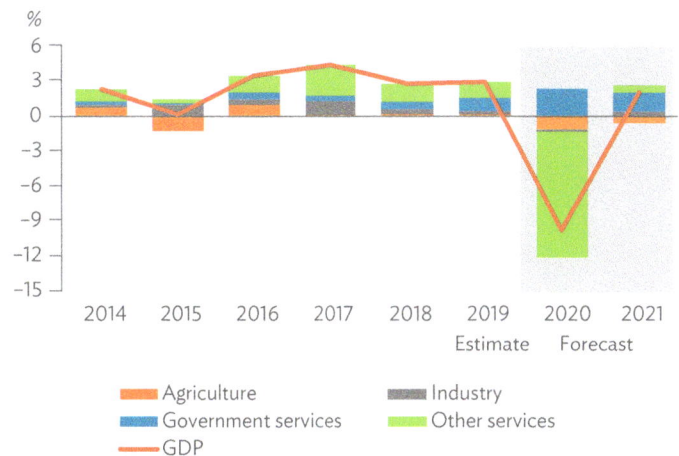

GDP = gross domestic product.
Sources: Vanuatu National Statistics Office; and Asian Development Bank estimates.

Vanuatu started the year with a comfortable level of international reserves. The Reserve Bank of Vanuatu reported that gross international reserves provided 13.1 months of import cover in May, well above its minimum threshold of 4 months. However, the current account deficit is expected to increase significantly in 2020 as tourism receipts decline in addition to the reduction in agriculture exports and remittances. Without increased development partner assistance, reserves are likely to fall.

Figure 18: Vanuatu Visitor Arrivals
(by mode of travel)

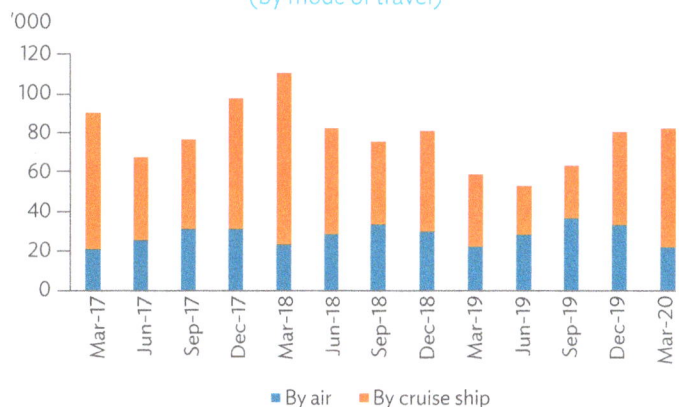

Source: Vanuatu National Statistics Office.

While lower commodity prices and the economic downturn will ease inflation pressures, supply chain disruptions because of COVID-19 and Tropical Cyclone Harold may counter this, pushing inflation higher. In response to COVID-19, the Reserve Bank of Vanuatu announced a reduction in the policy interest rate and the capital adequacy requirements of banks to support the economy (Figure 19).

Figure 19: Vanuatu Policy Interest Rate and Credit Growth

Source: Reserve Bank of Vanuatu.

The government's fiscal response to COVID-19 comprises two components equivalent to 4.8% of GDP in total: a Health Preparedness and Response Plan, announced on 12 March 2020, focused on containment measures and health system strengthening; and a fiscal stimulus focused on protecting jobs and stabilizing business activities. While the details of the fiscal stimulus package are being developed, it is expected to include employment stabilization payments, grants for affected small and medium-sized enterprises, agricultural price subsidies and transportation assistance, and educational grants and tuition fee subsidies.

Higher government spending on COVID-19 prevention and stimulus measures, combined with lower revenues, is expected to push the fiscal balance into a deficit in 2020. This would reverse the fiscal surpluses in 2018 and 2019, which averaged an estimated 7.2% of GDP. While revenue collections were above budget estimates for the first 3 months of the year, particularly from the Honorary Citizenship Programs, revenues from taxes and customs duties are expected to reduce as the economy contracts. Fiscal pressures, along with the rebuilding required following Tropical Cyclone Harold, could impact on public debt which was equivalent to 44.8% of GDP at the end of 2019, below the government's nominal debt ceiling of 60% of GDP.

References

ADB. 2020a. *Asian Development Outlook Supplement: Lockdown, Loosening, and Asia's Growth Prospects.* Manila.

ADB. 2020b. *Report and Recommendation of the President to the Board of Directors: Proposed Countercyclical Support Facility Loan and Grant to Solomon Islands for the COVID-19 Rapid Response Program.* Manila (Project Number 54178-001).

Food and Agriculture Organization of the United Nations (FAO). 2020. *The Pacific Islands: Tropical Cyclone Harold Situation Report May 2020.* http://www.fao.org/fileadmin/user_upload/emergencies/docs/Sit%20Rep_Cylone%20Harold_6May2020.pdf

International Monetary Fund. 2020. *Solomon Islands Request for Purchase Under the Rapid Financing Instrument and Disbursement Under the Rapid Credit Facility–Press Release; Staff Report; and Statement by the Executive Director for Solomon Islands.* Washington.

World Bank. 2020. World Development Indicators. https://data.worldbank.org/

COVID-19 and the Pacific

As the number of confirmed positive cases of coronavirus disease (COVID-19) soared in most parts of the world, Pacific developing member countries (DMCs), led by the smallest and least well-off, were able to keep the virus at bay as they moved urgently and decisively to restrict travel from countries affected by COVID-19. Despite the huge economic impact that Pacific DMCs will have to bear, there are several reasons why urgent action is the key to addressing COVID-19 in the Pacific.

First, a significant proportion of the population would be vulnerable, the level of noncommunicable diseases in Pacific populations is among the highest in the world, and experience has shown people with existing health issues are most susceptible to COVID-19 (Table 1).

Second, health systems in the Pacific, despite decades of investment and capacity building, remain weak (Table 2). An uncontrolled and soaring number of COVID-19 cases would immediately overwhelm and incapacitate these health systems, creating bigger problems for these countries. Third, the Pacific experienced a devastating measles epidemic in late 2019. Finally, the economic devastation that COVID-19 has created is well understood in a region that is dependent on its people as its largest and most valuable natural resource.

With high levels of noncommunicable diseases in the Pacific, the pandemic highlights the need for safe, nutritious, and affordable food. Restrictions imposed to curb the spread of COVID-19 have disrupted local and international food supply chains, which make resolving health-related problems even more urgent and serious.

Table 1: Pacific Developing Member Countries Pre-existing Health Conditions and Noncommunicable Diseases

	NCD Mortality Rate[a]	Tobacco Use[b]	Raised Blood Pressure[c]	Childhood Obesity[d]	Adult Obesity[e]
Cook Islands	...	26.6	22.3	32.2	55.9
Fiji	30.6	26.7	21.7	11.5	30.2
Kiribati	28.4	52.0	21.5	23.0	46.0
Marshall Islands	...	...	21.3	26.6	52.9
Micronesia, Federated States of	26.1	...	25.0	20.7	45.8
Nauru	...	52.1	20.5	33.2	61.0
Niue	...	15.0	24.2	29.5	50.0
Palau	...	23.7	22.9	31.4	55.3
Papua New Guinea	30.0	37.0	25.6	9.8	21.3
Samoa	20.6	28.9	24.0	21.7	47.3
Solomon Islands	23.8	37.9	22.0	4.3	22.5
Tonga	23.3	30.2	23.7	26.7	48.2
Tuvalu	...	48.7	23.7	27.2	51.6
Vanuatu	23.3	24.1	24.2	8.3	25.2
Pacific developing member countries (average)	**25.8**	**33.6**	**23.0**	**21.9**	**43.8**
Western Pacific Region[f]	**16.2**	**26.3**	**19.2**	**9.8**	**6.4**
World	**18.3**	**23.6**	**22.1**	**6.8**	**13.1**

... = data not available, NCD = noncommunicable disease.
[a] Probability of dying from any of cardiovascular diseases, cancer, diabetes, and chronic respiratory diseases between age 30 and exact age 70 (%, 2016 comparable estimates).
[b] Age-standardized prevalence of tobacco use among persons 15 years and older (%, 2018 comparable estimates).
[c] Age-standardized prevalence of raised blood pressure among persons aged 18+ years (systolic blood pressure of >140 mmHg and/or diastolic blood pressure >90 mmHg, 2015 comparable estimates).
[d] Prevalence of obesity among children and adolescents (5–19 years) (%, 2016 comparable estimates).
[e] Age-standardized prevalence of obesity among adults (18+ years) (%, 2016 comparable estimates).
[f] Western Pacific Region, which includes all Pacific developing member countries, based on World Health Organization definition.
Sources: World Health Organization. 2020. *World Health Statistics 2020*. https://www.who.int/gho/publications/world_health_statistics/2020/en/; and World Bank. 2020. *World Development Indicators*. https://data.worldbank.org/.

Table 2: Pacific Developing Member Countries Health Systems

Data Type	Universal Health Care Coverage[a]	Medical Doctors[b]	Nurses and Midwives[c]	Hospital Beds[d]
Cook Islands	...	14.1	67.4	63.0
Fiji	64	8.6	33.8	23.0
Kiribati	41	2.0	38.3	15.3
Marshall Islands	...	4.2	33.4	27.0
Micronesia, Federated States of	47	1.8	20.4	32.0
Nauru	...	13.5	76.6	50.0
Niue	...	...	125.0	...
Palau	...	14.2	72.6	48.0
Papua New Guinea	40	0.7	4.5	...
Samoa	58	3.4	24.9	10.0
Solomon Islands	47	1.9	21.6	14.0
Tonga	58	5.4	41.6	26.0
Tuvalu	...	9.1	42.6	56.0
Vanuatu	48	1.7	14.2	17.0
Pacific developing member countries (average)	**50**	**6.2**	**44.1**	**31.8**
Western Pacific Region[e]	**77**	**18.8**	**36.3**	**44.4**
World	**66**	**15.6**	**37.6**	**27.0**

... = data not available.

[a] Coverage index for essential health services (based on tracer interventions that include reproductive, maternal, newborn and child health, infectious diseases, noncommunicable diseases, and service capacity and access). It is presented on a scale of 0–100 (2017 comparable estimates).

[b] Density of medical doctors (per 10,000 population, 2010–2018 latest available data).

[c] Density of nursing and midwifery personnel (per 10,000 population, 2010–2018 latest available data).

[d] Density of hospital beds (per 10,000 population, 2010–2018 latest available data).

[e] Western Pacific Region, which includes all Pacific developing member countries, based on World Health Organization definition. For hospital beds, East Asia and Pacific is based on World Bank definition.

Sources: World Health Organization. 2020. *World Health Statistics 2020.* https://www.who.int/gho/publications/world_health_statistics/2020/en/; and World Bank. 2020. *World Development Indicators.* https://data.worldbank.org/.

Aside from weak health services, limited hand washing facilities, high population densities, and large household sizes compound the risk that the virus could spread quickly once it has a presence in Pacific communities. In urban settlements around the region, lack of safe water supply complicates efforts to use improved hygiene to fight COVID-19. In Papua New Guinea, for instance, hand washing can be a challenge in some communities.

To address COVID-19 and other human-to-human transmissible diseases, water, sanitation, and hygiene practices should reach the three major goals: universal access, efficiency, and sustainability. Some Pacific DMCs have low rates of access to basic water supply and sanitation services, far below the world average (Figure 1).

In the fragile energy scenario of small islands, Pacific power utilities must also be ready for the impact of COVID-19. Governments need to have contingency plans to protect the energy sector, as it is essential to sustain the basic public goods and health of the population. For instance, a simple power outage because of a broken transmission or distribution line to a hospital could lead to human tragedy. Power outages can also be a serious hurdle in the governments' efforts to communicate effectively and update its respective populations of the actions it is taking to mitigate the spread of the virus.

Figure 1: Basic Sanitation and Drinking Water Services, 2017

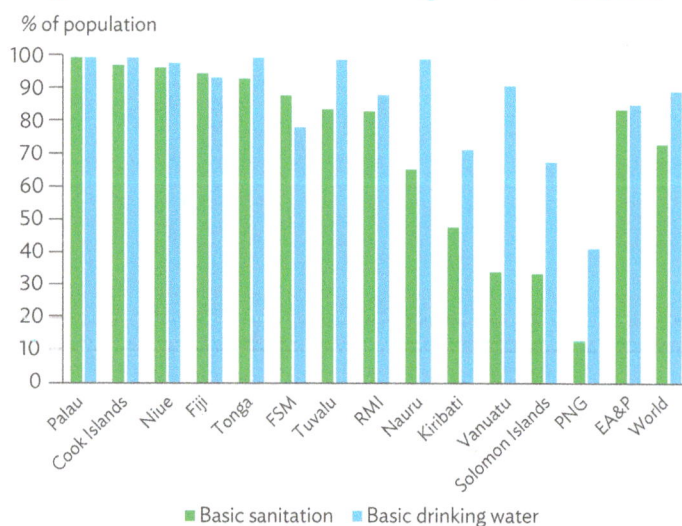

% of population

Basic sanitation   Basic drinking water

EA&P = East Asia and the Pacific, FSM = Federated States of Micronesia, PNG = Papua New Guinea, RMI = Republic of the Marshall Islands.
Source: World Bank. 2020. *World Development Indicators.* https://data.worldbank.org/; and World Health Organization and United Nations Children's Fund. 2020. *Water Supply, Sanitation and Hygiene (WASH) Database.* https://washdata.org/data.

Given its geographical layout, Pacific DMCs are also facing dual threat of COVID-19 and natural hazards. Fiji, Tonga, Solomon Islands, and Vanuatu were struck in early April by Tropical Cyclone Harold, which left dozens dead and thousands homeless. Emergency relief and evacuation operations were complicated by the need to observe physical distancing and other preventive measures. Reconstruction is expected to be hampered by trade and travel restrictions.

The dual threats highlight the need for the response to COVID-19 also to be a response to the climate crisis. Actions on resilience must be ramped up so that society can beat the COVID-19 crisis, while reducing the impact of climate threats. The pandemic demonstrates that disasters are triggered by multidimensional risks and hazards, and that a country's approach to urban resilience needs to be multifaceted.

With the increased use of face masks and other personal protective equipment, households are producing more household waste. Preventive and containment measures also lead to increased amounts of dangerous medical and other nonbiodegradable wastes. COVID-19 is changing the way we think about waste management. These changes must be managed for our immediate safety and for the long-term welfare of our communities.

Finally, the biggest impact of COVID-19 is the significant reduction in household incomes, and this requires immediate attention. Crafting small business solutions that are specific to country circumstances could help save millions of livelihoods in poor communities and fortify economies against future shocks. As an example, small businesses can be supported to reinvent their business models using new technologies. Governments can invest in satellite-based earth observation technology to provide smallholder farmers with continuous data on land and water resources. Satellite information on water levels and weather forecasts can help smallholder farmers reduce water stress and consumption, while raising yields by as much as 200%–250%.

While Pacific DMCs have been broadly successful in controlling the entry of the virus in the subregion, its governments must also be swift in responding to the challenges brought about by the painful but necessary decision to close borders and, consequently, a huge part of most of the economies. The immediate passage of supplementary budgets to provide much-needed economic stimulus is a step in the right direction, but it must be complemented by an equally fast implementation of the planned spending items to ensure quick recovery from this crisis.

Lead author: Prince Cruz

References

Abbasov, Rafael. 2020. *Are Pacific power utilities ready for the impact of COVID-19?* https://blogs.adb.org/are-pacific-power -utilities-ready-for-the-impact-COVID-19.

Bhandari, Preety and Arghya Sinha Roy. 2020. *The response to COVID-19 should also be a response to the climate crisis.* https:// blogs.adb.org/response-to-COVID-19-should-response-to -climate-crisis.

Galing, Edkarl and Alexandra Conroy. 2020. *In Papua New Guinea, hand washing can be a challenge in some communities.* https://blogs.adb.org/in-papua-new-guinea-hand-washing -can-be-a-challenge-in-some-communities.

Huang, Jingmin. 2020. *Water, sanitation and hygiene key to Pacific's ongoing COVID-19 strategy.* https://blogs.adb.org/blog/ water-sanitation-and-hygiene-key-to-pacific-s-ongoing -covid-strategy.

Jain, Anupma. 2020a. *Dual threat in the Pacific: COVID-19 and natural hazards.* https://blogs.adb.org/dual-threat-in-the -pacific-COVID-19-and-natural-hazards.

Jain, Anupma. 2020b. *In the Pacific, COVID-19 is changing the way we think about waste management.* https://blogs.adb.org/ in-the-pacific-COVID-19-changing-way-we-think-waste -management.

Siddiq, Akmal. 2020. *COVID-19 highlights the need for safe, nutritious, and affordable food.* https://blogs.adb.org/blog/ covid-19-highlights-need-safe-nutritious-and-affordable -food.

Schou-Zibell, Lotte. 2020. *Small business solutions for pandemic challenges.* https://blogs.adb.org/small-business -solutions-for-pandemic-challenges.

Veve, Emma. 2020. *In the Pacific, urgent action is the key to addressing COVID-19.* https://blogs.adb.org/blog/pacific -urgent-action-key-addressing-covid-19.

Making choices: Pacific health systems and the COVID-19 pandemic

The Pacific region was largely protected from the surge in COVID-19 cases as the pandemic spread across the world during the first half of 2020. As of 23 July 2020, only two Pacific developing member countries had reported cases (Fiji with 27 and Papua New Guinea with 30). The limited spread of the disease across the Pacific was because of the inherent geographical remoteness of island countries and their ability to effectively shut borders early in the pandemic. Only Papua New Guinea shares a land border, and thus has to continuously manage the risk of cross-border infections. While the low infection rates in the Pacific region indicate that the region has successfully controlled the spread of COVID-19 (thus far), the impact of the pandemic on Pacific health system is likely to have significant long-term negative consequences, if decisions on resource allocation are not carefully considered.

Uncertainty in the health sector is a constant challenge for resource allocation as many health events and crises occur unexpectedly. This uncertainty is heightened during a pandemic, which is both fast spreading and poorly understood. The COVID-19 pandemic has forced decision makers globally to make trade-offs between the health of populations and other sectors, especially the economy. Because of global shortages of test kits and limited testing capacity in Pacific countries, data on COVID-19 incidence in the subregion is sparse. This lack of information on disease incidence, together with generally weak health information systems (including an incomplete picture of the health system infrastructure preparedness), can lead to poor short-term decisions instead of a more comprehensive and coherent approach to resource allocation for long-term development.

Health systems vary in performance across the Pacific, with some having successfully addressed critical maternal and child health and infectious disease concerns, while others are only just recovering from recent communicable disease outbreaks. A common feature across Pacific health systems is the lack of adequate hospital infrastructure, including beds, isolation units, and respiratory units. For COVID-19 testing, most Pacific developing member countries remain dependent on overseas support for diagnostic capacity (Table 1). Without being able to test and treat, Pacific populations are at elevated risk of COVID-19 morbidity and mortality. The early shutdowns have largely prevented these negative health events; however, in most cases, health systems have not been strengthened to cope with future possible infection waves.

COVID-19 health impact and costs will be unevenly spread with increased mortality and poorer clinical outcomes among those in the older age group (65 years and over) as well as those with

Table 1: Pacific Health System Capacity Indicators

Pacific DMC	Current Hospital Bed Capacity	Estimated Beds Required in Case of Local COVID-19 Transmission[a]	COVID-19 Testing Capability
Cook Islands	170	348	Overseas (New Zealand); local (in calibration)
Fiji	1,800	17,670	Local (FCCDC)
Kiribati	175	2,317	Overseas (FCCDC); local (in calibration)
Marshall Islands	150	1,168	Overseas (US CDC); local
Micronesia, Federated States of	360	2,253	Overseas (US CDC); local
Nauru	55	254	Overseas (FCCDC)
Niue	8	32	Overseas (New Zealand)
Palau	80	358	Overseas (TCDC, US CDC); Local
Papua New Guinea	900	172,126	Overseas (Australia); local
Samoa	250	3,923	Overseas (Australia); local
Solomon Islands	610	13,057	Overseas (Australia); local (in calibration)
Tonga	300	2,064	Overseas (Australia); local (in calibration)
Tuvalu	50	230	Overseas (FCCDC); local (in calibration)
Vanuatu	500	5,854	Overseas (Australia); local

COVID-19 = coronavirus disease, DMC = developing member country, FCCDC = Fiji Centre for Communicable Disease Control, TCDC = [Taipei,China] Centers for Disease Control, US CDC = United States Centers for Disease Control and Prevention.

[a] Projections are based on current populations of Pacific countries, and an assumed 10% infection rate given current preparedness measures; 20% of those infected will require hospitalization, 5% of hospitalizations will be severe and require ventilators.

Sources: Asian Development Bank estimates; National government official health and COVID-19 websites.

co-morbidities (diabetes and hypertension). With adult obesity prevalence ranging from 30% in Fiji to over 60% in Nauru and with one of the highest diabetes rates in the world (prevalence of 40%), the subregion potentially faces an additional health burden from COVID-19 infection (Table 1, page 26). Moreover, the current travel restrictions in place adds an additional barrier to those seeking tertiary health care overseas that, otherwise, are not available in-country.

Indirect costs from COVID-19 will continue into the long term. The majority of Pacific health systems are weak, with inadequate investment and almost total reliance on public financing. With reduced government revenues because of COVID-19—latest estimates show that tax revenues are on track to fall short of pre-pandemic budget projections across most Pacific countries by at least 10% up to as much as over 45% this year—health budgets can expect to be cut in line with overall government budgets. While some Pacific countries have earmarked public financing for COVID-19-related response, this has largely been reallocations within the health sector budget. The reallocation is particularly concerning when it depletes resources away from other critical health priorities like HIV and tuberculosis or immunization programs. A drop in access and service delivery for infectious diseases (medication, treatment, immunizations, etc.) can result in future outbreaks. On the demand side, populations might reduce their health-seeking behavior for fear of being infected with COVID-19 when visiting hospitals, which might then reduce critical health programs, such as pre and antenatal care, diabetes management, and chronic disease screenings for breast and cervical cancer.

Pandemic response units have been established in some Pacific countries with the aim of increasing the speed in decision-making, particularly around procurement and testing. However, in some cases, this has led to bypassing the established procurement and supply systems. Medical supply chain systems are already fragile in most countries, and the recent influx of supply donations has often been arranged outside of the health sector, but with the expectation that the health sector would be responsible for distribution and absorption (including adequate training for proper use of personal protective equipment (PPE), and adaptation for new testing protocols and equipment). Excess equipment and supplies that are donated without going through the domestic medical standard lists risk not being used and will increase the burden of medical waste or even misuse, leading to elevated risk of infection, especially if not managed. Established regional supply chain systems are severely affected by the sharp reduction of international freight options, posing significant challenges for logistics, with some countries having not had vaccines shipment for more than 3 months.

Health systems require a healthy workforce to function effectively. However, with a lack of adequate PPE, health workers are themselves at increased risk of contracting COVID-19, especially in the Pacific with an ageing health workforce. The result of shortages of supplies and poor communication from governments has resulted in some health staff not reporting for work. Needless to say, a health system cannot function effectively without a well-trained workforce. Chronic shortages of health workers have been also a recurrent issue in the Pacific. For instance, Vanuatu reported that more than 50 health facilities were forced to shut between 2017 and 2020 because of lack of health workers.

Resource allocation under COVID-19 has raised efficiency questions in the health system with parallel systems and misaligned procurement and distribution. Also, there are equity concerns with the elderly and those without access to handwashing being more vulnerable to poorer health outcomes, if they become infected and at greater risk of spreading the infection. Some have raised gender concerns with potential reduction in antenatal services and outreach care because of reduced mobility and lack of health workers. With weak and incomplete health information systems and limited capacity to analyze data, policymakers and planners risk making poor decisions about the allocation of resources.

Appropriate interventions in the Pacific to prevent COVID-19. Social distancing, while proven effective in many countries, may not work in the Pacific region where different social and family constructs prevent its effectiveness. Families often live together in multigenerational homes. Transport is expensive and car ownership low, with most people moving around in crowded buses or even small boats. As seen elsewhere, there is a lack of understanding on the externalities of infectious diseases, making it harder for people to place general public health safety ahead of their personal immediate needs, such as getting food, going to work, or running errands. In some countries, which are still experiencing a significant communicable disease burden from tuberculosis, malaria, or HIV, people may feel less of a sense of fear of the spread of COVID-19.

Concluding Remarks

While Pacific countries appear to have avoided the immediate increased mortality and morbidity burden from COVID-19, their weak health systems are likely to be impacted in the long run from erosion of routine services, resulting in poorer population health outcomes. Decision-making around limited resource allocation is not a unique challenge to the Pacific, but with limited capacity, data, and information, and donors providing supplies outside of the health system, there is a real risk that the pandemic will further weaken health systems and overall population health will likely decline because of reduced health-seeking behavior and availability of comprehensive essential health care services. Development partners and governments need to ensure that, when responding to a pandemic, they do not erode recent gains in health system strengthening. Including economists in developing pandemic response plans and budget allocations will also facilitate resource allocation decisions for the short, medium, and long term. Clear communication from the government to populations and rural health workers on pandemics will work to mitigate any possible decline in quality of services and health-seeking behaviors.

Governments and development partners will need to address the socioeconomic impacts of the pandemic, determine gaps in the data available to effectively respond to the needs, and take policy actions to mitigate or address the impacts where possible. This includes continuing to build health systems' capacity to contain and manage imported cases should a large-scale community outbreak occurs. In the immediate term, prioritization may be given toward making sure that health care workers are kept safe through adequate provision of PPE and up-to-date infection control and prevention training, risk communication, and community engagement activities. The prioritization is needed to minimize disruption to essential public health services and address negative health-seeking behaviors. Focus must be directed also toward having protocols on social distancing, clinical management, and repatriation to reduce preventable mortality and adverse social and economic impact of COVID-19, including non-pharmaceutical interventions at workplaces, schools, and mass gatherings, such as churches and feasts. In the medium- to-longer-term recovery, governments should be encouraged to allocate resources toward building the resilience of the health system for disasters and emergencies, such as enhancing surveillance capacities to detect early signs, becoming less dependent on external support for critical public health functions, and minimizing vulnerabilities to the socioeconomic impact of health crises.

Lead authors: Inez Mikkelsen-Lopez and Ki Fung Kelvin Lam

Poverty and the pandemic in the Pacific

The coronavirus (COVID-19) has had a far greater economic than health impact in the Pacific. The Asian Development Bank's (ADB) May 2020 estimates suggest that the effects of lockdowns and travel bans will be a fall in gross domestic product of almost 10% in Pacific developing member countries[1] (ADB 2020), even though, at the time of writing, there have been fewer than 50 confirmed cases of COVID-19 (Johns Hopkins University 2020) in the subregion. This significant downturn in economic activity is likely to reduce household incomes throughout the subregion, and push hundreds of thousands of people into poverty. This brief examines this issue by presenting scenarios about what the potential, short-term country-level impacts of COVID-19 will be on poverty in the Pacific. Our results suggest that, if policymakers do not provide substantial transfers to households, the number of people living in extreme poverty in the subregion could increase by up to 40% in the short-term.

Methodology

We consider two scenarios—10% and 20% fall in household consumption—to illustrate how large the potential short-term economic contraction caused by COVID-19 might be, and look at what this means in terms of the number of people living in poverty. These scenarios correspond with forecasts produced by international organizations (ADB 2020 and OECD 2020). However, at this stage, no one knows for sure how large the negative economic impact of COVID-19 will be because it depends on how long it takes for economic activity to resume as normal. As such, we believe it is prudent to consider a range of possibilities. This is especially the case given that some growth forecasts, particularly those by the International Monetary Fund (2020), have received considerable criticism for being overly optimistic (e.g., Sandefur and Subramanian 2020).

To estimate the effect of these contraction scenarios on poverty, we draw on the World Bank's online database of poverty statistics that are based on Household Income and Expenditure Surveys (World Bank 2020). We use an augmented poverty line approach, whereby we inflate the value of the poverty line to a level that corresponds with the poverty line following a contraction and calculate the headcount. For example, to determine the increase in poverty of a contraction of 10% in individuals' consumption, we inflate the value of the poverty line, say $1.90 a day to $2.11[2] a day, then calculate the headcount ratio at this line. We explain the methodology in detail in our United Nations University World Institute for Development Economics Research Working Paper (Sumner, Ortiz-Juariz, and Hoy 2020). It is similar to the approach used by researchers at the World Bank who produce global estimates of the potential short-term increase in poverty from COVID-19 (Mahler et al. 2020).

We consider the impact of these contraction scenarios on the share of the population living below $1.90, $3.20, and $5.50 a day (in purchasing power parity (PPP) 2011 dollars) in the 10 countries in the Pacific where data are available[3]. These poverty lines correspond with internationally accepted definitions of extreme poverty ($1.90), the median national poverty line in lower middle- income countries ($3.20) and the median national poverty line in upper middle-income countries ($5.50) (Jolliffe and Prydz 2016).

Existing levels of poverty

To simplify the discussion, we divide the 10 Pacific countries with data available into three groups based on their development status and on the level of poverty that existed prior to COVID-19.[4] The first group consists of the larger fragile states, Papua New Guinea (PNG), Timor-Leste, and Solomon Islands, where about a quarter of the population lived below $1.90 a day and over 75% of people lived on less than $5.50 a day. These rates of extreme poverty are already higher than any country in Asia, and are about half of the average for Sub-Saharan Africa (World Bank 2020). Collectively, these three countries are home to more than 97% of the extremely poor people in the subregion and over 80% live in PNG alone (Figure 1).

Figure 1: Share of the Population Living in Extreme Poverty in the Pacific by Country

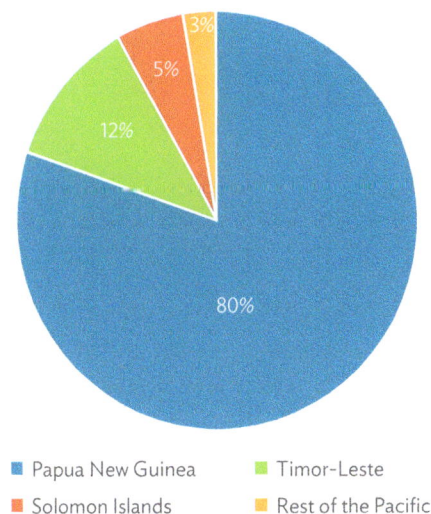

- Papua New Guinea
- Timor-Leste
- Solomon Islands
- Rest of the Pacific

Note: ADB moved Timor-Leste from the Pacific to the Southeast Asia country grouping in 2019.
Source: World Bank. 2020. PovcalNet. http://iresearch.worldbank.org/PovcalNet/data.aspx

The second group of countries, all of which hold lower middle-income status, comprises Vanuatu, Kiribati, and the Federated States of Micronesia (FSM). About 10%–15% of the population live below $1.90 a day and 65%–75% live on less than $5.50 a day in these countries. This level of poverty is slightly above the average for Asian countries (World Bank 2020).

Extreme poverty is rare[5] in the third group of countries—Fiji, Tonga, Samoa, and Tuvalu—all of which have upper middle-income status. These countries have some of the lowest rates of extreme poverty in Asia (World Bank 2020). However, between 25% and 35% of the population in these countries still live below $5.50 a day.

Potential increases in poverty

The scenarios we present in Figure 2 suggest that the number of people living in extreme poverty in the Pacific may increase rapidly because of the impact of COVID-19. If countries in the subregion experience a 10% contraction in household consumption, the share of the population living below $1.90 a day is set to increase to over 30% of the population in the first group of countries and to between 14% and 19% in the second group of countries. Under this scenario, extreme poverty would re-emerge in the remaining countries, with the number of people living below $1.90 a day more than doubling. If a more severe contraction of a 20% fall in household consumption occurs, an additional 1.2 million people in the subregion would be pushed into extreme poverty, resulting in an increase of about 40% on pre-COVID-19 levels. The impact will be especially sizable in PNG where hundreds of thousands of people would be pushed into extreme poverty and Timor-Leste where a large share of the population lived just above the $1.90 (2011 purchasing power parity) line prior to the outset of COVID-19.

The impact of COVID-19 on poverty at higher lines, specifically $3.20 and $5.50 a day, will be somewhat smaller as large shares of the population of the Pacific already live below these lines. In the case of PNG, Timor-Leste, and Solomon Islands, a 10% contraction would result in 58%–76% of the population living below $3.20 a day (compared with 53%–70% pre-coronavirus) and 83%–95% of the population living below $5.50 a day (compared with 78%–93% pre-COVID-19). Under this scenario, almost half of the population would live below $3.20 a day and three-quarters would live below $5.50 a day in the second group of countries (Vanuatu, Kiribati, and the FSM). While in Fiji, Tonga, Samoa, and Tuvalu, about 10% of the population would live below $3.20, and about 40% of the population would live below $5.50 a day if a 10% contraction will occur. A 20% contraction would lead to over 60% of the population in the subregion living below $3.20 a day, and over 80% living below $5.50 a day.

These estimates point to the fact that there are large shares of the population who live just above the poverty lines in the Pacific and that they are vulnerable to falling below it. The scenarios we present are based on potential contractions in household consumption brought about by COVID-19. However, any shock, such as a natural disaster, could have a similar impact. The reality is that the vast majority of people in the subregion who have escaped poverty are still far from having a secure "middle class" living standard. Studies suggest that, to permanently escape poverty, people need to live on more than $10 a day (López-Calva and Ortiz-Juarez 2014). The share of the population living above this line is as small as 1% in Timor-Leste, 3.5% in Solomon Islands, and 5.5% in PNG, and as high as 34.5% in Tonga, 32.5% in Samoa, and 27% in Fiji (World Bank 2020).

Policy implications

Policymakers can mitigate these dramatic short-term increases in poverty through the provision of direct consumption support to households. A total of 171 countries have adopted over 800 social protection measures to minimize the impact of COVID-19 on households (Gentilini et al. 2020). However, many governments in the Pacific have yet to implement these. Timor-Leste is an exception because, in response to COVID-19, the government has provided cash transfers to all households that live on less than $500 a month (Magalhães 2020).

There is encouraging evidence from the few instances where governments in the Pacific have provided transfers directly to households to help mitigate the negative economic consequences of a crisis. For example, in Fiji, following widespread devastation caused by Tropical Cyclone Winston, the national government provided additional payments to the poorest 10% of households. Importantly, these households were already part of the formal social protection system in Fiji so it was relatively straightforward for the government to provide them with a transfer. An impact evaluation of this emergency response payment showed that, 3 months after the cyclone took place, beneficiaries were more likely to have recovered from the shocks they faced, relative to comparable households that did not receive the additional assistance (Mansur et al. 2018). This includes having recovered from sickness or injury, repaired their dwelling, replenished their food stocks, remedied the damage to their agricultural land, and repaired village or neighborhood infrastructure.

Relative to the rest of world, there is a notable absence of formal social protection systems in the Pacific, which makes it much harder to provide transfers to poorer households quickly in response to an economic shock (World Bank 2018). A key lesson from the current crisis for policymakers in the subregion is that establishing and/or expanding the coverage of social protection systems that are targeted toward the poorest households in their country will ensure that, when the next economic shock hits, large segments of the population do not fall back into poverty. Even when countries are not facing a crisis, social protection payments still have an important role to play. Global evidence suggests that over a third of the poor who were included in their country's social protection system were able to escape extreme poverty (World Bank 2018).

Figure 2: Share of the Population Living in Poverty under a 10% and 20% Economic Contraction

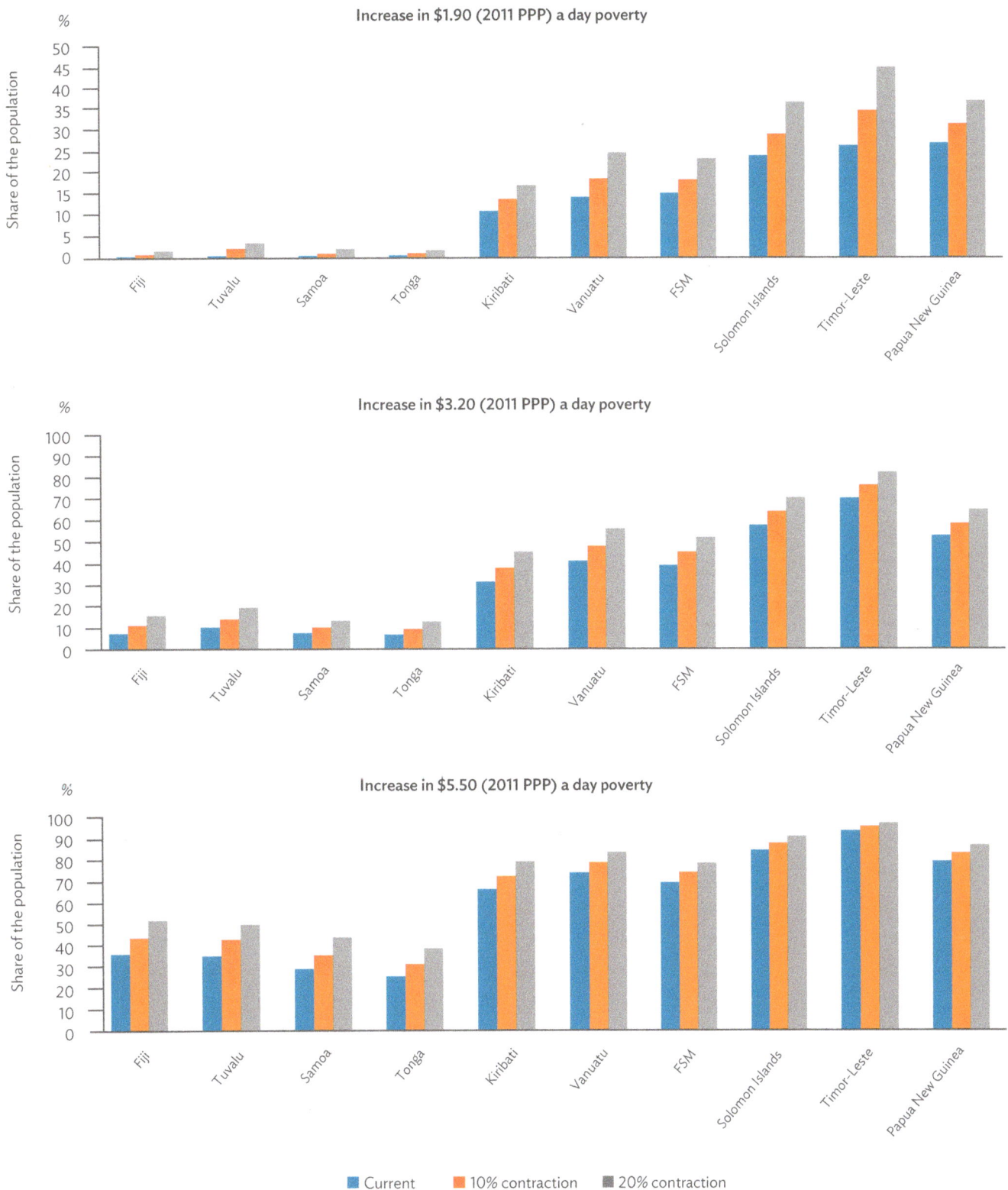

FSM = Federated States of Micronesia, PPP = purchasing power parity.
Note: ADB moved Timor-Leste from the Pacific to the Southeast Asia country grouping in 2019.
Source: Author's estimates using data from World Bank. 2020. PovcalNet. http://iresearch.worldbank.org/PovcalNet/data.aspx

Appendix Table: Share of the Population Living in Poverty under Each Scenario
(%)

Country	$1.90			$3.20			$5.50		
	2018	10% Fall	20% Fall	2018	10% Fall	20% Fall	2018	10% Fall	20% Fall
Fiji	0	1	2	7	11	16	36	43	52
Kiribati	11	14	17	31	38	45	66	72	79
FSM	15	19	24	39	45	52	69	74	78
Papua New Guinea	27	32	37	53	58	65	79	83	86
Samoa	1	1	2	8	10	13	29	35	44
Solomon Islands	24	29	37	58	64	70	84	87	90
Timor-Leste	27	35	58	70	76	82	93	95	97
Tonga	1	1	2	7	9	13	25	31	38
Tuvalu	1	2	4	10	14	20	35	43	50
Vanuatu	14	19	25	41	48	56	74	78	83

Note: ADB moved Timor-Leste from the Pacific to the Southeast Asia country grouping in 2019.
Source: Author's estimates using data from World Bank. 2020. PovcalNet. http://iresearch.worldbank.org/PovcalNet/data.aspx

Lead author: Christopher Hoy, Research and Policy Fellow, Crawford School of Public Policy, Australian National University

Endnotes

[1]   ADB Pacific developing member countries include: the Cook Islands, Fiji, Kiribati, Marshall Islands, the Federated States of Micronesia, Nauru, Niue, Palau, Papua New Guinea, Samoa, Solomon Islands, Tonga, Tuvalu, and Vanuatu. ADB moved Timor-Leste from the Pacific to the Southeast Asia country grouping in 2019. In this policy brief, Pacific includes Timor-Leste as it is one of the countries being monitored by the Australian National University Development Policy Center.

[2]   This figure is calculated by dividing $1.90 by 0.9. More details are provided in in our United Nations University WIDER Working Paper (Sumner, Ortiz-Juariz, and Hoy 2020).

[3]   There are five ADB developing member countries in the Pacific that were not included because of a lack of data being available. These are the Cook Islands, the Marshall Islands, Nauru, Niue, and Palau.

[4]   The most recent year for which comparable data are available across countries is 2018.

[5]   Only 1%–2% of the population live below $1.90 a day.

References

Asian Development Bank (ADB). 2020. An Updated Assessment of the Economic Impact of COVID-19. *ADB Briefs No. 133*. Manila.

Gentilini, U., M. Almenfi, P. Dale, J. Blomquist, R. Palacios, V. Desai, and V. Moreira. 2020. Social Protection and Jobs Responses to COVID-19: A Real-Time Review of Country Measures. *Living paper version 9*. Washington, DC: World Bank (15 May).

International Monetary Fund (IMF). 2020. *World Economic Outlook, April 2020: The Great Lockdown*. Washington, DC.

Johns Hopkins University. 2020. *Coronavirus Resource Center*. Baltimore.

Jolliffe, D. and E. Prydz. 2016. Estimating International Poverty Lines from Comparable National Thresholds. *World Bank Policy Research Working Paper 7606*. Washington DC.

López-Calva, Luis F. and E. Ortiz-Juarez. 2014. A Vulnerability Approach to the Definition of the Middle Class. *Journal of Economic Inequality* 12 (1): 23–47.

Magalhães, Fidelis. 2020. Timor-Leste's COVID-19 state of emergency is a twin effort to save people's lives and their livelihoods. *The Diplomat*.

Mahler, D. G., C. Lakner, R. A. Castañeda Aguilar, and H. Wu. 2020 The impact of COVID-19 (Coronavirus) on Global Poverty: Why Sub-Saharan Africa might be the Region Hardest Hit. *World Bank Blogs*. Washington, DC (20 April).

Mansur, A., J. Doyle, and O. Ivaschenko. 2018. Cash Transfers for Disaster Response: Lessons from Tropical Cyclone Winston. *Development Policy Centre Discussion Paper* No. 67.

Organisation for Economic Co-operation and Development (OECD). 2020. *OECD updates G20 summit on outlook for global economy*. Paris.

Sumner, A., E. Ortiz-Juarez and C. Hoy. 2020. Precarity and the pandemic: COVID-19 and poverty incidence, intensity, and severity in developing countries. *UNU-WIDER Working Paper* 2020/77. Helsinki: United Nations University World Institute for Development Economics Research (UNU-WIDER).

Sandefur, J. and A. Subramanian. 2020. The IMF's Growth Forecasts for Poor Countries Don't Match Its COVID Narrative. *CGD Working Paper* 533. Washington, DC: Center for Global Development.

World Bank. 2018. *The State of Social Safety Nets 2018*. Washington, DC.

World Bank. 2020. *PovcalNet*. http://iresearch.worldbank.org/PovcalNet/data.aspx

Pursuing fiscal reform amid the COVID-19 pandemic in Papua New Guinea

A government-mandated *Papua New Guinea Taxation Review* released in 2015 characterized the tax system of Papua New Guinea (PNG) as (i) too reliant on personal income and salary and wage tax; (ii) having a narrow tax base contributing to relatively high corporate and personal income tax rates; (iii) guided by outdated legislation that lacks clarity; (iv) overuses tax incentives on a discretionary basis; (v) overly generous in use of stability contracts in resource development projects; and (v) using a tax administration system not well suited for business growth and development.

Under the COVID-19 pandemic, the treasurer has announced that the country will face a revenue shortfall equivalent to 2.7% of gross domestic product (GDP) in 2020, which could raise the projected fiscal deficit from 5.0% to 8.4% of GDP unless expenditure cuts are instituted. Without expenditure cuts, borrowing to finance the deficit is projected to push public debt above the current legislatively allowable ceiling of 45% of GDP. This adds impetus to the revenue reform process, as well as exerts further pressure on the government's ability to manage debt, which is already challenged by (i) arrears, (ii) contingent liabilities, (iii) debts of state-owned enterprises (SOEs), and (iv) managing risks related to rolling over external and domestic borrowings.

This article examines some of the policy challenges faced by PNG's tax system, as highlighted by the 2015 Taxation Review, and of its debt portfolio. It also looks into the progress made in addressing revenue and debt issues, including the role played by development partners.

Papua New Guinea's tax revenue mobilization challenge

PNG has one of the lowest tax-to-GDP ratios in the East Asia and Pacific region (Figure 1). Overall revenue (tax and non-tax, excluding grants) as a percentage of GDP has averaged 17.9% between 1999 and 2013, but since has reached a low of 13.4% in 2016 (Figure 2). Since 1999, tax revenue (i.e., on income, profits, international trade, and goods and services) averaged 16.0% of GDP, reaching a high of 20.7% in 2004 and a low of 12.5% in 2016. Non-tax revenue has been quite volatile as a percentage of GDP, from a low of 0.3% in 2013, to 2.2% in 2018, and averaging at 1.2%.

PNG's tax-to-GDP fluctuations are characterized by volatile revenue receipts from the resources sector. In 2009–2011, revenue from minerals accounted for more than 20% of total revenue (excluding grants), mostly supported by oil production. In 2013, the country received a $19 billion investment in extraction and processing of liquefied natural gas, which boosted revenues from corporate income tax, personal income tax, and goods and services tax in the non-mineral sectors linked to the construction of the pipeline and liquefaction plant. However, the construction period concluded in 2013 and in 2014, PNG was hit with the shock from

a fall in mineral commodity prices. Thus by 2016, revenues linked to mineral production accounted for only 4% of total revenue. Subsequently, the government has struggled to diversify its revenue base beyond dependence on the mineral sector.

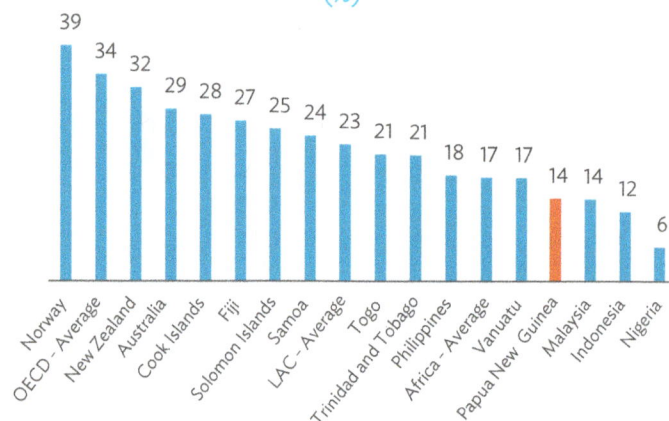

Figure 1: Tax-to-Gross Domestic Product Ratios, 2017 (%)

LAC = Latin America and the Caribbean, OECD = Organisation for Economic Co-operation and Development.
Source: Organisation for Economic Co-operation and Development.

Figure 2: Papua New Guinea Revenues
% of gross domestic product

Sources: Organisation for Economic Co-operation and Development, Government of Papua New Guinea, and Asian Development Bank estimates.

Reliance on income taxes leads to high income tax rates. In 2018, 43.4% of total revenue came from income taxes (Table 1). It is also estimated that over 90% of personal income tax[1] was contributed by salary and wage taxes paid by just 400,000 people in the formal workforce—4.8% of the national population. Discretionary incentives, described in the next section, have narrowed the tax base, and the government has found it difficult to reduce income tax rates in a falling tax-to-GDP ratio environment.

Personal income tax rates in PNG range from 22% of taxable income up to 42%, divided into five income tax slabs. The average effective tax rate (i.e., total tax paid divided by income) for annual incomes equivalent to $10,000 is 20% in PNG compared with Fiji's less than 5% for the same amount.[2] The income tax slabs were last revised in 2018, when the tax-free threshold was raised and the real tax burden on the lowest-income band reduced. However, the average tax rate in PNG is still one of the highest in the Pacific region.

Figure 3: Trends in the Benchmark Corporate Tax Rate

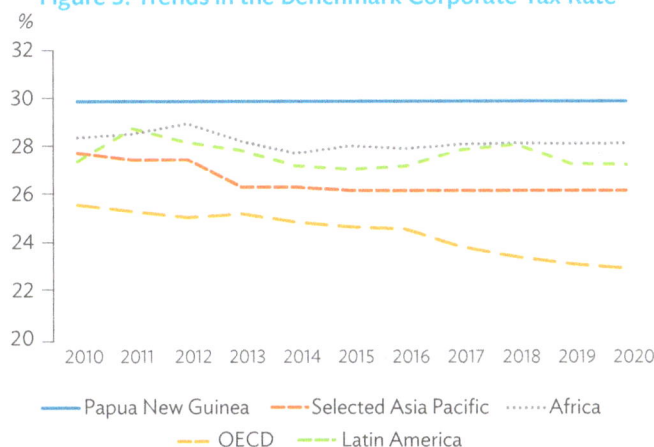

OECD = Organisation for Economic Co-operation and Development.
Note: Selected countries in Asia and the Pacific comprises Australia, Indonesia, Fiji, the Philippines, and Samoa.
Sources: Organisation for Economic Co-operation and Development; and KPMG. Corporate Tax Rates Table. https://home.kpmg/xx/en/home/services/tax/tax-tools-and-resources/tax-rates-online/corporate-tax-rates-table.html (accessed: 19 June 2020).

Discretionary tax incentives and high corporate tax rate. Figure 3 shows the trend of the benchmark rate for corporate income tax on resident companies worldwide. PNG's tax rate for nonresident companies was as high as 45% in some sectors until 2017. The resident corporate income tax rate of 30% (uniform now for most resident and nonresident companies since 2017) is still higher than the average rate for Asia (21.0%) and globally (23.8%).[3]

However, many companies qualify for discretionary tax incentives. These are exemptions from the payment of tax that have been granted on a discretionary basis to "qualifying" companies. As of 2019, 25 tax incentives were available in PNG directly on corporate income.[4] Incentives include additional deductions on investments in primary production activities, exempt income on qualifying export products, and additional deductions granted in the tourism and agriculture sectors. In most cases, the qualifying criteria are non-transparent and rarely audited. Further, the incentives were granted without offsetting measures to protect government revenue.

Outdated, unclear tax legislation. PNG's prevailing Income Tax Act, containing all principal statutes and relevant administrative provisions, was enacted in 1959. Subsequent, successive amendments using different drafting styles and terminologies have caused the original structure to be lost and the law to become increasingly complex, uncertain, and difficult to comprehend. In its current form, the legislation lists a number of tax concessions even before establishing the tax that is payable.

Administrative provisions are also difficult to decipher as administrative rules are drafted into the main legislation. Put together, the complexity of legislation has bled into tax administration and the lack of clarity has stalled disputes, debt collections, and other matters of administration. PNG's ranking for ease of paying taxes

Table 1: Revenue Share from Various Sources
(share of gross domestic product, 2018)

Country	Total Revenue	Tax Revenue	Income, Profits, and Capital Gains Tax			Goods and Services Tax	International Trade Tax	Non-tax Revenue	% of Income Tax in Total Revenue
			Personal Income	Corporate Income	Other				
Cambodia	22.2	17.2	0.9	3.2	0.0	10.7	2.4	5.1	18.5
Fiji	27.0	24.2	1.7	3.3	1.6	12.4	5.2	2.8	24.6
Malaysia	16.1	12.0	2.3	6.0	0.0	3.1	0.3	4.4	51.2
Palau	42.8	20.4	3.7	0.0	0.0	10.6	5.3	23.3	8.6
Papua New Guinea	19.9	14.8	4.4	3.9	0.4	5.0	1.1	5.1	43.4
Philippines	16.3	14.7	2.2	3.4	0.3	4.4	3.4	2.5	36.5
Samoa	29.2	23.8	3.1	2.1	0.0	15.8	2.7	5.5	17.9
Solomon Islands	42.0	29.6	4.5	4.8	0.0	6.2	13.6	12.9	22.2
Thailand	17.4	14.7	1.7	4.3	0.0	8.0	0.6	2.8	34.4
Timor-Leste	49.0	4.8	0.6	1.3	0.0	2.1	0.7	44.2	4.0
Vanuatu	38.5	17.8	0.0	0.0	0.0	13.6	3.7	21.2	0.0

Source: International Monetary Fund Government Finance Statistics, 2018.

in the World Bank's Doing Business Index deteriorated from 109th out of 190 countries in 2018 to 118th out of 190 countries in 2020. This situation is especially problematic as PNG moves toward self-assessment, where taxpayers themselves estimate their payable tax. To ensure that proper taxes are paid, the guiding legislation must be simple enough for the average citizen to understand.

Incentives in the mining and petroleum sector. The 2015 Taxation Review noted that the tax arrangements for PNG's mining and petroleum sectors (prior to 2017) were generous compared with other resource-rich countries and did not reflect the maturity of the PNG resource sector. The review notes that project agreements were in conflict with existing laws requiring changes to legislation for them to be applicable and are kept under strict confidentiality, besides containing stabilization and nondiscriminatory clauses, authorized under the Resource Contracts Fiscal Stabilisation Act 2000. The country's largest, state-owned mine, Ok Tedi, has its own governing law, the Ok Tedi Act 1976; and another significant nickel and cobalt mine, the Ramu Nickel project, operates under a special mining lease with a 10-year tax holiday and exemption from import duties. Mineral exports are also exempt from the goods and services tax, and this status was extended to suppliers/contractors of the designated resource projects until recently. Table 2 summarizes PNG's fiscal regime for mining, petroleum, and gas.

Although legislative changes in 2017 significantly standardized the regime governing these resource projects, there is still a risk of granting contract-based exemptions that undermine the main tax legislation. Since these contracts are granted, all incoming investment in PNG hopes to acquire the same terms as previous projects. Thus, the reforms need to be supported by a political willingness to refrain from signing contracts that are significantly different from the suggested regime in the legislation.

The current tax holidays and concessions granted to some of the large resource projects and a low commodity price environment may mean that, until at least 2025 when the liquefied natural gas project is expected to begin realizing profits, resource revenues will remain subdued keeping PNG from building fiscal resilience to shocks.

Notes on Papua New Guinea's public debt

The issues discussed in the previous section limit the government's capacity to generate sufficient revenues to fund its expenditures, resulting in fiscal deficits that must then be covered by borrowing. The stock of the central government's debt stood at K33.6 billion (equivalent to 39.8% of GDP) at the end of 2019, up from K30.2 billion (38.3% of GDP) a year earlier (Tables 3 and 4). The increase was mainly because of "extraordinary" budget support loan facilities

Table 2: Fiscal Regime for Mining, Petroleum, and Gas Sectors in Papua New Guinea

Tax Type		Mining	Petroleum	Gas	Other Sectors
Company income tax	Pre-2017	30% (resident), 40% (nonresident)	50% (oil fields), 45% (standard), 30% (incentive)	30%	30% (resident), 48% (nonresident)
	Post-2017	30% (resident)	30% (resident)	30%	30% (resident)
Dividend withholding tax	Pre-2017	10%	Exempt	Exempt	17%
	Post-2017	15%	15%	15%	15%
Interest withholding tax	Pre-2017	0%	15% (domestic, foreign companies exempt if lending to resource industry)	15% (domestic, foreign companies exempt if lending to resource industry)	15%
	Post-2017	15% (exemption repealed)	15% (exemption repealed)	15% (exemption repealed)	15%
Goods and services tax		Zero rated	Zero rated	Zero rated	10%
Contractors withholding tax	Pre-2017	12%	Not applicable	Not applicable	17%
	Post-2017	15%	15%	15%	15%
Royalties and levies		2.25% (copper, gold)	2% (royalty on wellhead value[a] + 2% development levy)	2% (royalty on wellhead value + 2% development levy)	
Thin cap. debt to equity ratio		3:1	3:1	3:1	2:1
Carry-forward of tax losses	Pre-2018	Indefinitely	Indefinitely	Indefinitely	20 years
	Post-2018	20 years	20 years	20 years	7 years
Additional profits tax	Pre-2017			Two tier rate of return : 17.5%/20% thresholds with, 7.5%/10% rates	
	Post-2017	15% (threshold), 30% (rate)	15% (threshold), 30% (rate)	15% (threshold), 30% (rate)	15% (threshold), 30% (rate)

Thin cap. = Thin capitalization.
[a] Overall royalty was 2% because royalty on well head was considered an advance payment on corporate tax.
Source: Department of Treasury. Various years. Income Tax Act, 1959 (compiled by the Asian Development Bank).

Table 3: Papua New Guinea Debt Stock as a Share of Gross Domestic Product, 2019–2022
(K million)

	2018	2019	2020		2021	2022
	Actual	Actual	Budget	Post-COVID-19		
Domestic debt	17,103.3	19,333.5	19,640.4	20,691.7	21,867.4	21,867.4
% of gross debt	*58.7%*	*57.4%*	*52.8%*	*52.9%*	*50.4%*	*50.4%*
External debt	12,017.8	14,333.4	17,545.2	18,422.8	21,562.6	21,562.6
% of gross debt	*41.3%*	*42.6%*	*47.2%*	*47.1%*	*49.6%*	*49.6%*
Gross government debt (i.e., arrears)	**29,121.1**	**33,666.9**	**37,185.6**	**39,114.5**	**43,430.0**	**43,430.0**
Debt to GDP %	**35.4%**	**39.8%**	**40.3%**	**48.0%**	**47.6%**	**47.6%**
Arrears	*2,623.0*	*1,982.0*	*930.0*	*930.0*	*0.0*	*0.0*
Gross government debt - with arrears	*31,744.1*	*35,648.9*	*38,115.6*	*40,044.5*	*43,430.0*	*43,430.0*
Debt to GDP % (incl. arrears)	*38.6%*	*42.2%*	*41.3%*	*49.1%*	*47.6%*	*44.2%*

COVID-19 = coronavirus disease, GDP = gross domestic product.
Source: Government of Papua New Guinea, Department of Treasury. 2020. *2020 National Budget, Volume 1*. Port Moresby.

from multilateral institutions[5] and drawdowns from the proceeds of the government's inaugural 10-year sovereign bond. It was also brought about by (i) inclusion of cross-currency valuation effects on debt (i.e., the result of valuation of loans payable in foreign currencies using end-year exchange rates), (ii) inclusion of outstanding domestic arrears, and (iii) recognition of portions of contingent liabilities.[6] The share of outstanding government domestic debt in total public debt at the end of 2019 declined to 57.4% from its previous year of 58.7%, and is projected to further decline to 52.9% in 2020, consistent with the government's Medium-Term Development Strategy 2018–2022 to lower domestic interest costs and restructure domestic debt portfolio to longer maturities, with a view to lower risk of refinancing from domestic sources.

The government plans to fund its relatively large financing requirement, estimated to be 6.6% of GDP[7] for the 2020 budget through further reliance on concessional financing both from bilateral sources (Government of Australia for further budget support) and multilateral sources (use of the World Bank Development Policy Operation budget support facility, Asian Development Bank [ADB] budget support facilities and the International Monetary Fund [IMF] rapid credit facility). The government has also released new COVID-19 -related domestic bonds to cover some of the financing requirements in 2020.

The added pressure from the COVID-19 pandemic. The above financing plans may change, subject to the evolving pandemic. As with most economies around the world, the pandemic is having a multidimensional impact on the PNG economy. The economy is expected to contract significantly, not only as the result of contraction of activities because of the government imposed restrictions on travel and social distancing regulations, but also on account of declining commodity prices and weaker demand for PNG's exports. The government faces a balance-of-payments financing gap of up to 4% of GDP because of reduced current account surplus, which is only partially mitigated by lower financial account outflows.[8] Government revenues are also expected to decline even as emergency health expenditures as well as social and economic support expenditures rise significantly.

In April, the government announced a K5.6 billion economic stimulus package that includes K500 million in additional fiscal spending in 2020, a K600 million credit line negotiated with commercial banks to support businesses, and K500 million made available by superannuation funds to employees affected by the economic slowdown.[9] The remaining amount in the stimulus package refers to the additional financing raised by the government through additional domestic market borrowing (K2.5 billion in COVID-19 treasury bonds) and concessional credit accessed through the IMF Rapid Credit Facility (K1.5 billion). These much-needed steps will adversely impact the government's debt-servicing capacities in the short term. The limited scope of the 15 April 2020 Group of 20 announcement regarding suspension of debt services to bilateral creditors can alleviate the government's 2020–2023 debt service vulnerabilities, but only to some extent.

The 9 June IMF approval to disburse $363.6 million in emergency financing will help the government address the urgent balance-of-payments needs created by COVID-19. However, although the country has relatively few COVID-19 cases thanks to the government's swift containment efforts, the IMF's latest debt sustainability analysis suggested that PNG is at high risk of external and overall public debt distress under a prolonged impact of the pandemic or another export earning shock.

Other important challenges to managing public debt. The Government of PNG has been incorporating domestic arrears into its public debt profile and plans to extinguish them by 2022. However, the exact levels of debt faced by SOEs have yet to be determined, as these are not being monitored at this time. In his budget speech, the minister of the Treasury Department rightly said that "the financial challenges facing many of these SOEs will only worsen … when expensive debt repayments fall due."

Contingent liabilities have remained high, although their exact levels also have yet to be determined. Last year, the Department of Treasury estimated these at K14.1 billion, 91.0% of which are guarantees extended to external creditors. In the past, servicing of both principal and interest costs of some guaranteed loans had become a burden on the budget. With the absence of any risk management procedures, such risks are not currently lower, and indeed these contingent commitments can haunt the budget in future years.

Status of reforms

Improving revenue outcomes. The Medium-Term Revenue Strategy (MTRS) 2018–2022 operationalizes the comprehensive 2015 Taxation Review and, more recently, recommendations made by the IMF's annual reviews. It seeks to initiate revenue mobilization in PNG by overcoming the issues that have historically plagued the tax environment.

The MTRS envisions reducing income tax rates in PNG without forgoing revenue in the process. Thus, offsetting measures to improve revenue in the MTRS include crawling back some of the tax incentives and introducing a capital gains tax. The government also instituted a review aimed at rationalizing the tax incentive system. Further since 2018, the government has published a tax expenditure statement as part of the national budget to improve transparency on the use of tax incentives.

Some of the most important progress in revenue reforms comes in the changes to the income tax legislation. Under the MTRS, the country has legislated a separate Tax Administration Act in 2017, although this has yet to be implemented. Also, it has nearly finished drafting a new income tax act with technical assistance from the IMF, using modern terminology appropriate for a self-assessment regime.

Reducing public debt. Besides working to dial down current expenditure and strengthen SOEs oversight to improve efficiency, both of which would help reduce the need to borrow especially when faced with a shrinking resource envelope, government efforts to directly rein in its debt include (i) establishing an interagency office under the Department of Treasury to monitor and clear arrears; and (ii) working to include "elements that were previously excluded," such as contingent liabilities, into public debt reporting. Including contingent liabilities in total public debt will not only enhance

transparency in government reporting and allay part of the concerns about debt data completeness, but it could also lead to improved credit ratings as well. Also, the Department of Treasury has begun sharing with the Bank of Papua New Guinea detailed projections for debt payments, receipts, and cash to improve debt planning.

Support from development partners. Development partners have supported the Government of PNG, mostly through technical assistance, in implementing crucial public financial management reforms. In February 2020, the IMF approved a Staff-Monitored Program to help PNG correct structural imbalances and address fiscal and monetary issues, including the continued implementation of the MTRS toward gradually reducing public debt.

Although progress in meeting some program targets may be delayed because of the COVID-19 pandemic, others have been met and the government remains committed to the program. It has set specific milestones to be achieved within 2020. These include passing the new income tax act into legislation, which would be implemented beginning in 2021 together with the Tax Administration Act; and conducting reviews to determine the best institutional arrangements for collecting tax and customs revenues, as well as to crafting an improved dividend policy for SOEs.

Conclusion

PNG's current revenue system has been limiting the government's capacity to generate sufficient revenues to fund its expenditures, at times forcing the government to introduce successive supplementary budgets and, at other times, resorting to additional domestic and external borrowing to cover its fiscal deficits. Although the government has been forced to deviate from its debt strategy and request parliamentary approval to raise the threshold level of debt to GDP (now set at 45%), it has been mindful of the sustainability of its revenue and public debt and plans to implement its current MTRS and Medium-Term Debt Strategy. Now, with COVID-19 and its inevitable budgetary implications, the government's current approach to rely on donor concessional financing and adherence to the IMF Staff-Monitored Program is very much critical and prudent.

Lead authors: Abhimanyu Dadu and Gholam Azarbayejani, consultants, Papua New Guinea Resident Mission

Endnotes

1   Government of Papua New Guinea, Department of Treasury and ADB estimates.

2   ADB estimates.

3   KPMG. *Corporate Tax Rates Table*. https://home.kpmg/xx/en/home/services/tax/tax-tools-and-resources/tax-rates-online/corporate-tax-rates-table.html (accessed: 19 June 2020).

4   Government of Papua New Guinea, Department of Treasury. 2019. *2019 National Budget, Volume 1*. Port Moresby.

5   Disbursements from concessional loan financing, originally budgeted for at K816.9 million rose to K1,311.7 million, mainly from ADB projects Civil Aviation Investment Program, Highlands Region Roads Improvement Program, and Sustainable Highlands Highway Investment Program.

6   Of more than 10 loan guarantees, the government has recognized three domestic loans, the debt services for which have been made from the budget. At the end of 2019, the outstanding balance for these loans amounted to K1,176 million.

7   ADB staff estimated fiscal deficit in 2020.

8   IMF staff report attached with the *Request for Disbursement Under the Rapid Credit Facility* estimates a current account surplus to reduce from 22% of GDP pre-pandemic to 14.6% of GDP post-pandemic.

9   There is no indication of whether the commercial bank credit facility and superannuation fund disbursement are guaranteed by government revenue at this time.

References

Government of Papua New Guinea, Department of Treasury. 2020. *2019 Final Budget Outcome*. Port Moresby.

International Monetary Fund. 2017–2019. *Article IV Consultation – Staff Report*. Washington, DC.

International Monetary Fund. 2020. *Request for Disbursement Under the Rapid Credit Facility – Staff Report*. Washington, DC.

World Bank. 2020. *Doing Business 2020*. Washington, DC.

Nonfuel Merchandise Exports from Australia
(A$; y-o-y % change, 3-month m.a.)

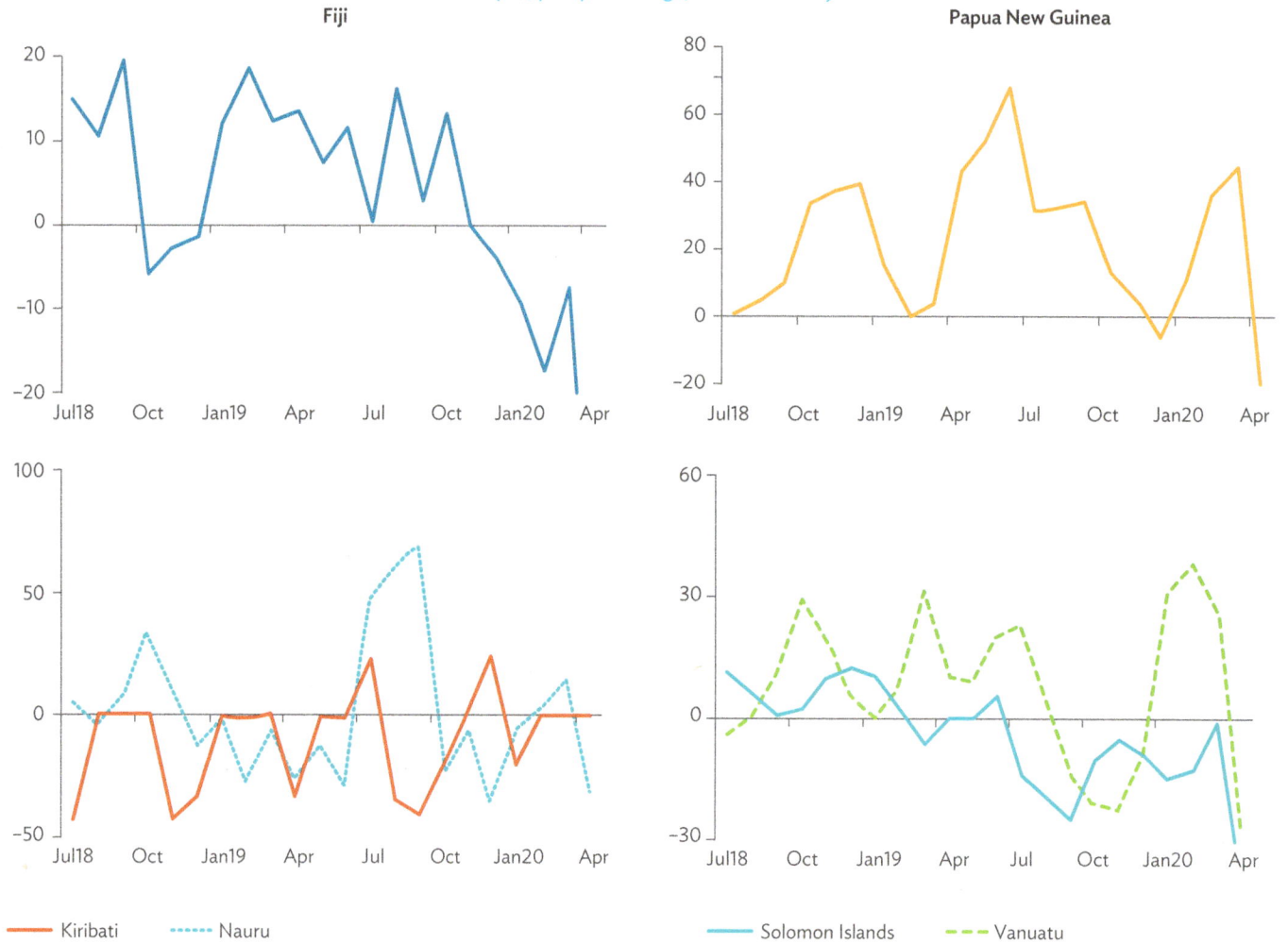

Fiji

Papua New Guinea

Kiribati ———   Nauru ·······

Solomon Islands ———   Vanuatu - - - -

A$ = Australian dollars, lhs = left-hand scale, m.a. = moving average, rhs = right-hand scale, y-o-y = year-on-year.
Source: Australian Bureau of Statistics.

Nonfuel Merchandise Exports from New Zealand and the United States
(y-o-y % change, 3-month m.a.)

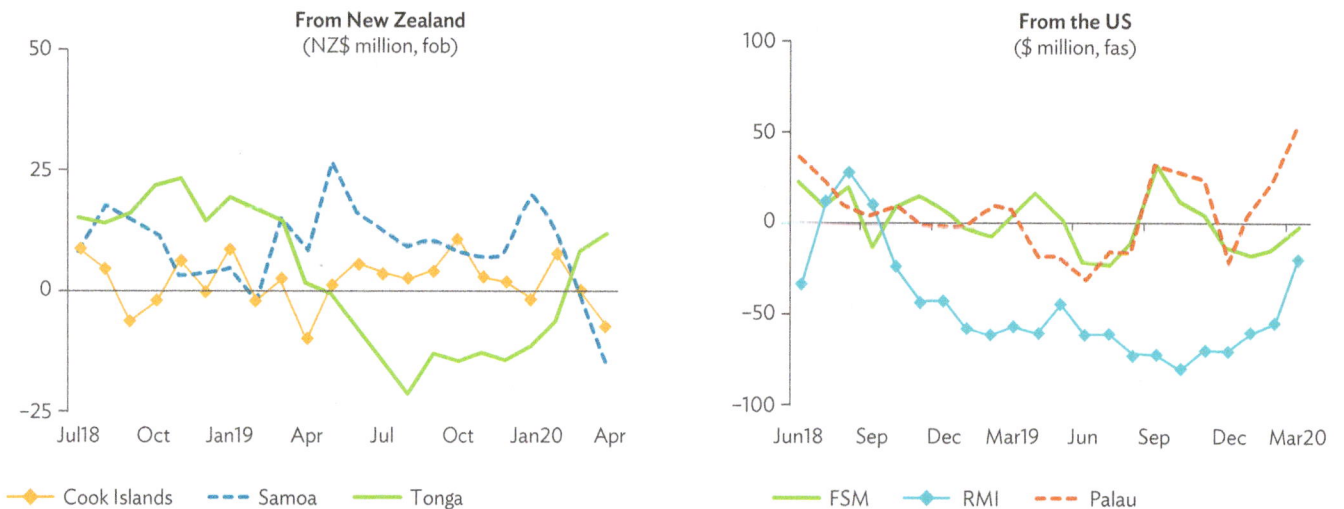

From New Zealand
(NZ$ million, fob)

From the US
($ million, fas)

Cook Islands ———   Samoa - - - -   Tonga ———

FSM ———   RMI ———   Palau - - - -

fas = free alongside, fob = free on board, FSM = Federated States of Micronesia, m.a. = moving average, NZ$ = New Zealand dollar, RMI = Republic of the Marshall Islands, US = United States, y-o-y = year on year.
Sources: Statistics New Zealand and US Census Bureau.

Diesel Exports from Singapore
(y-o-y % change, 3-month m.a.)

Fiji

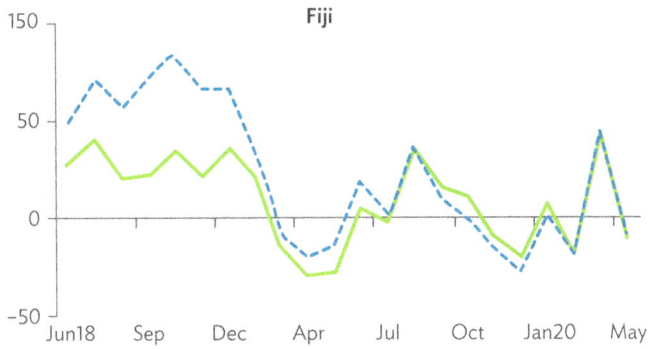

Papua New Guinea

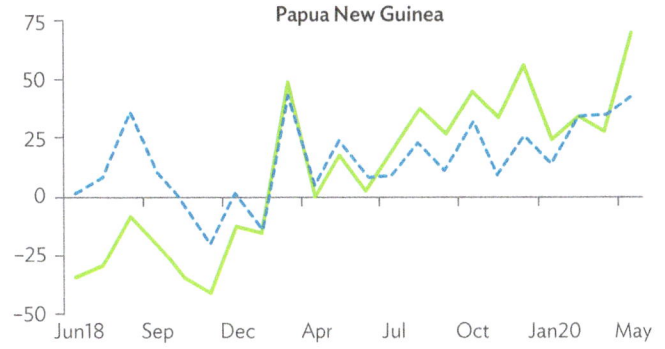

Samoa

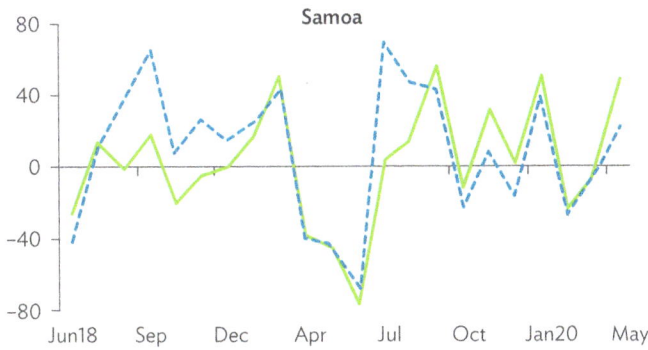

Solomon Islands

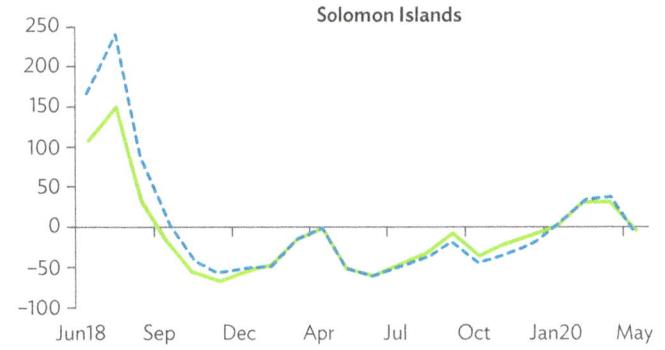

—— Volumes   - - - Values

m.a. = moving average, y-o-y = year on year.
Source: International Enterprise Singapore.

Gasoline Exports from Singapore
(y-o-y % change, 3-month m.a.)

Fiji

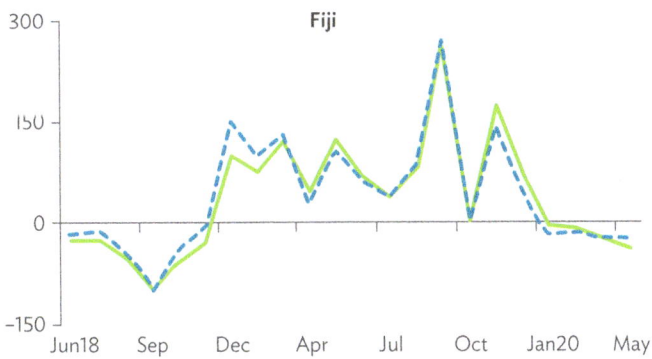

Papua New Guinea

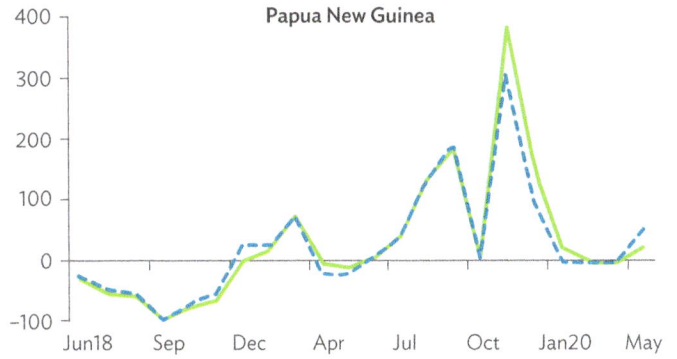

Samoa

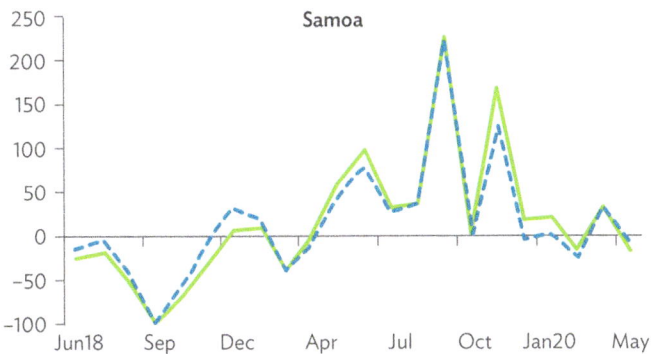

Solomon Islands

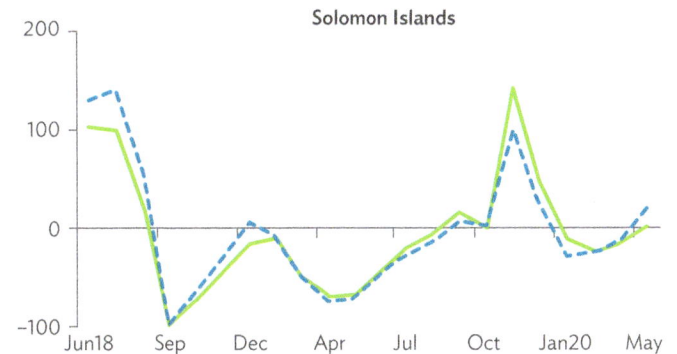

—— Volumes   - - - Values

m.a. = moving average, y-o-y = year on year.
Source: International Enterprise Singapore.

Departures from Australia to the Pacific
(monthly)

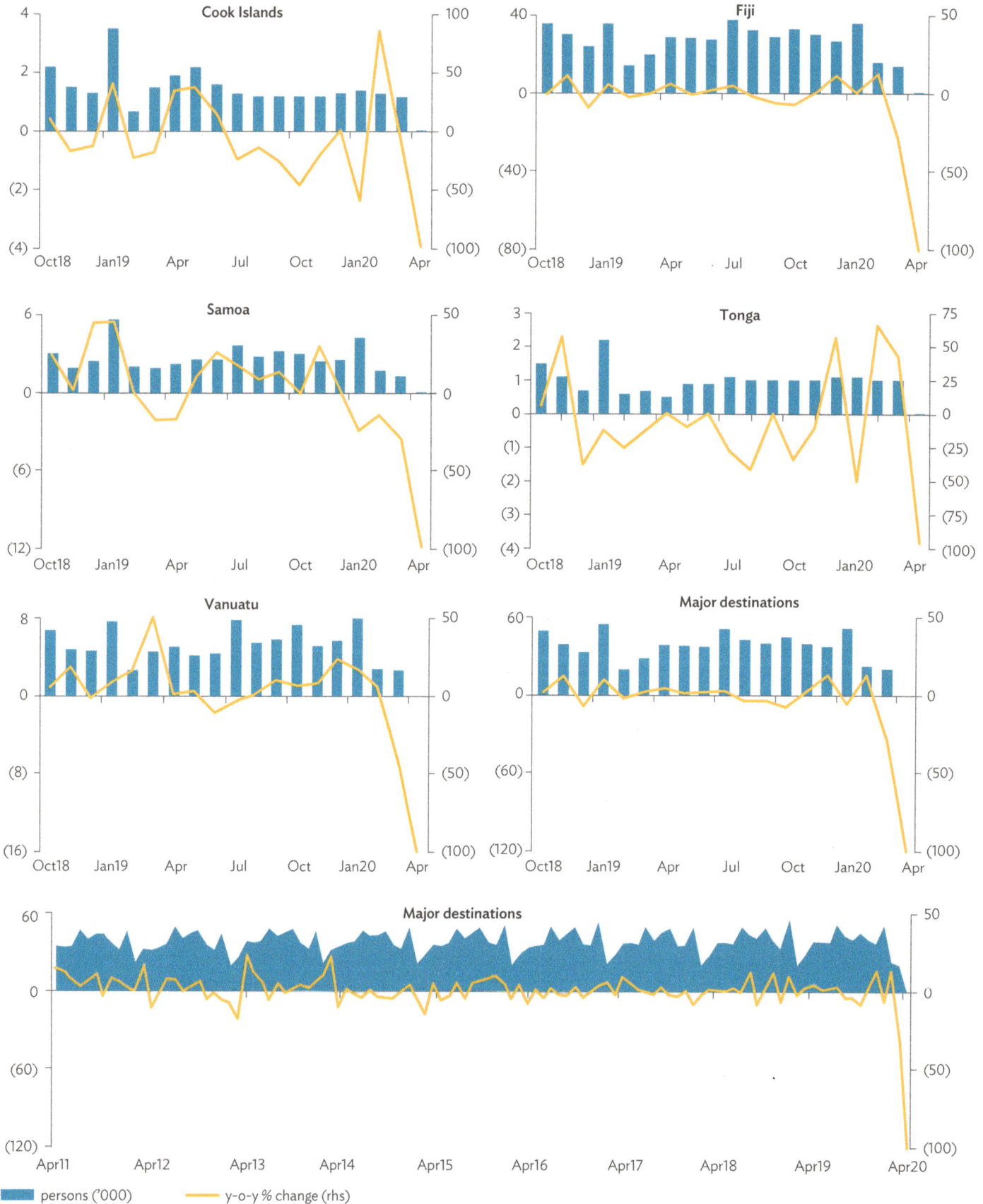

Cook Islands

Fiji

Samoa

Tonga

Vanuatu

Major destinations

Major destinations

persons ('000)　　　y-o-y % change (rhs)

rhs = right-hand scale, y-o-y = year on year.
Source: Australian Bureau of Statistics.